PENGUIN BOOKS

GARDEN UP

Ekta is a researcher turned entrepreneur living in Mumbai. She spent a decade studying Ecology, ranging from soil nutrient dynamics in the forests of southern India to sustainable farming practices among communities in the Himalayas.

After finishing her PhD from the prestigious Indian Institute of Science, Bengaluru, she decided to make a career in digital media and edutainment through her own venture, Garden Up, a logical extension to a very successful Youtube channel.

Today, Garden Up content, services and products, cater to a wide-ranging Indian and international audience, helping them find greenery, sustainability and balance in their lives. You can find out more about her work at https://www.gardenup.in/

GARDEN UP

*Your one-stop guide to
growing plants at home*

DR EKTA CHAUDHARY

PENGUIN BOOKS

An imprint of Penguin Random House

PENGUIN BOOKS

USA | Canada | UK | Ireland | Australia
New Zealand | India | South Africa | China

Penguin Books is part of the Penguin Random House group of companies
whose addresses can be found at global.penguinrandomhouse.com

Published by Penguin Random House India Pvt. Ltd
4th Floor, Capital Tower 1, MG Road,
Gurugram 122 002, Haryana, India

Penguin
Random House
India

First published in Penguin Books by Penguin Random House India 2022

ISBN 9780143452447

Typeset in Sabon LT Std by Manipal Technologies Limited, Manipal
Printed at Thomson Press India Ltd, New Delhi

www.penguin.co.in

To the memories of my childhood

CONTENTS

Part III: Bonus Unlocked

INTRODUCTION

Here's an idea: The real reason why Adam and Eve were banished from the Garden of Eden was because they weren't doing a good job of tendering it. Sounds ridiculous? Here's another one: Merely looking at plants can heal patients. Now, before you slam the book shut, this one is a fact, backed by solid scientific evidence from studies on actual patients #sciencefacts. So, bringing flowers for the sick during hospital visits isn't that silly after all! Whether you are a believer of biblical stories or a hardcore rationalist, if you are reading this book, I will bet on one of two things: (1) You are sold on the idea of home gardening but have developed cold feet, or (2) You have already killed a plant. Either way, this book will tell you how to not be an Adam.

During the 1980s, the National Aeronautics and Space Administration (NASA) funded a study to find solutions for long-term habitation in closed environments meant to be used in space. In 1989, Dr B. Wolverton, the lead scientist on the study, published his work concluding, 'If man is to move into closed environments, on Earth or in space, he must take along nature's life support system.' If you haven't guessed already, the solution he was offering were plants. He also published a list of plants capable of removing air pollutants, such as benzene, xylene, carbon monoxide and formaldehyde, commonly found in homes around the world. A few decades later, our beloved capital, New Delhi, was choking on thick clouds of smog. As Delhi's air quality reached hazardous levels and stayed there for days, people started looking for solutions and rediscovered Dr Wolverton's list. Social media caught on and spread it like wildfire. Blogs were written, videos were made (admittedly, your author's first million view video was also on the topic), nurseries changed some labels, and these 'air purifying' plants went off shelves in a matter of days.

The fact that all this was happening in the national capital made it newsworthy, possibly making it yet another serious wake-up call for my generation to a form of conscious living. Before that, an affinity for organic and healthy food had become largely well-entrenched. I believe this trend is able to sustain itself because of two factors. First, as opposed to the previous generation, this generation is born in times of sufficiency. So, understandably, their focus has shifted from necessity to quality. Second, the quality of resources, be it air, water or food, has drastically deteriorated, thanks to the pressures of exploding demand. And then came the

COVID 19 pandemic, a once-in-a-century phenomenon with the ability to force us into a completely different lifestyle. Every sign so far tells us that many who survive this pandemic will embrace this trend of conscious living, if anything, more strongly than before. Many among us will also become a part of a growing breed of home gardeners, whether to improve the quality of air we breathe, to be aware of the food we eat, to pick a worthy new hobby or to teach our kids a valuable lesson in patience.

What I am going to share in this book is not pathbreaking, but it is put together for a purpose. Having been on this journey, my hope is to help you get there sooner. This book is a crash course on building an intuition about plants. I start with an assumption that my readers are constrained by space and time. I will rely on logic and basic science to narrate my experiences, not as a protocol but as a story, so that the next time you see a yellowing leaf, a white bug on your hibiscus or a money plant cutting that refuses to grow, you will know exactly what's going on, what you need or where to look.

At a very basic level, to read and understand this book, all that you need to know at the start is that plants use carbon dioxide from the air, water from the soil to make food in the presence of sunlight. Their food is primarily sugars, which they circulate in their body and utilize for their growth. This simple (actually not-so-simple) process is responsible for supporting the entire human civilization, right from fossil fuels formed over centuries to the food we eat.

But assuming that you bought this book because you are already sold on the idea of how important plants are for humans and you would like to know more on how to care for them and where you could be going wrong, then, my fellow gardener, don't be worried because you are not alone. Here, I will share my personal experiences, recommendations on what plants to grow and where to grow them along with some fun science facts. I will share not only the 'how to' of gardening but also the 'why' of it—why are leaves green in colour, why do we take a cutting, why can't I water that plant daily or why do I need to water this plant daily.

I will try my best in this book to not make it feel like a boring biology class. But there are some very important basics that anyone thinking of getting plants needs to be made aware of. As I make relevant recommendations for different levels of gardeners, I will also highlight some common varieties of each plant that are easily available in the Indian subcontinent, for the geographical conditions of India and neighbouring countries. Through my YouTube content on Garden Up, I have also found these tips and tricks to work not only in India but also for gardeners from Pakistan, Nepal, Bangladesh, Philippines, Vietnam and even the global Middle East.

I have divided the book into three parts such that each part and each chapter within those parts can be read

independently. The first chapter is for readers who wake up one day and decide to start gardening with absolutely no background. It talks about the bare minimums, the frills and the alternatives. I'll talk about the sun, temperature, nutrients, water, soil and tools. The guiding principle here is that **it's not about what you need, but what your plants need.** The second chapter is a collection of the most common 'how tos' for gardening, right from taking a cutting to fixing insect problems. If you picked this book hoping to find quick answers to your specific doubts, I suggest you start by looking at this chapter.

The next part of the book is dedicated to plants the way you and I see them. Of the ~3,91,000 plant species known to science, home gardeners, I think, need to know just two types: plants that are grown for their aesthetics (ornamental plants) and those that are grown for a specific output (utility plants). For the guiding principle in this part of the book, I'll turn the one in Part 1 on its head. When it comes to use, **it's all about what you need from that plant, and not what the plant needs.** Is it the green luscious leaves? Its colourful flowers? Its fruits or its roots? Through each chapter in these parts, we will cover the most common varieties available, why you should grow that plant, how to propagate that plant, common issues a home gardener may face, ways to deal with those problems, and a pro-tip from my personal experience with that plant (look for 'Super tip'). Throughout these chapters, our framework has just one scale of reference: the plant's use. In addition, where possible, I try to provide simple classifications and explanations about why plants fall in those categories. If gardening sounds simple already, then we are on to something.

In the chapter part titled 'Ornamental Plants', there are two main sections: the first on foliage plants and the second on flowers. In Section 3.1 on foliage plants, I will start with dismantling the commonly misunderstood distinction between indoor vs outdoor plants. I will then go on to establish the idea that the key determining factor in these plants' growth and health is the availability of natural light.

In Section 3.2 on flowers, I will highlight that the most important factor that a home gardener should consider for such plants is the timing and pattern of flowering. With the right conditions, jasmines can flower throughout the year in India, but if you are expecting a petunia to flower in July, you will be disappointed.

Under utility plants, I start by acknowledging that the risk (and disappointments) of failure is much higher than in the case of ornamental plants. In Section 4.1 as well, I classify edibles as seasonals and perennials. Section 4.2 covers ten plants, with known evidence of medicinal value that anyone can grow in the Indian subcontinent.

Towards the end of the book in Part III, we have three short, bonus chapters. Chapter 5 is dedicated to garden planning, things one needs to consider before spending any money or time on gardening. Chapter 6

is a collection of common terms that anyone is likely to encounter on their gardening journey. And finally, Chapter 7, is dedicated to gardening for kids, where I share three gardening projects for kids. These are further categorized based on the level of patience required, ranging from low to high.

I hope you enjoy your gardening journey. Lets Garden Up!

PART I

It's Not About What You Need
But What Your Plant Needs.

PART I

It's Not About What You Need
But What Your Plant Needs

Chapter 1
PLANT BASICS

Land plants came into existence on this planet more than 800 million (80 crores) years before humans did. They had it all figured out before we arrived. They also grow in the wild on their own and do just fine. Then why do they need to be cared for in a home garden?

The reason is simple: because they may not be growing in their actual habitat where they have evolved to survive, and if at all they happen to be growing in their native geography, they might be in a plastic pot in a living room next to the air conditioner where, their microenvironment will be completely different despite being in the city where they have grown for thousands of years. Microenvironment is the immediate environment around the plant, and it is made up of factors like the availability of sunlight, water, humidity, etc.

Additionally, plants, especially trees, can develop roots which are 30 ft or deeper over several decades to access groundwater even when no one waters them intentionally. That's certainly not possible in a suburban highrise of Mumbai.

#FUNFACT: *Deepest root system ever documented so far is of Shepher's tree (Boscia albitrunca), with roots going deeper than 70 metres in the Kalahari Desert. Trees growing in dry regions invest in deep roots to access scarce groundwater. This is a feature that helps them sustain long dry spans when there is no drop of rain for months.*

So, what does a plant need? Primarily water, sun and nutrients! Each plant has a different requirement for these three resources. An experienced gardener (or social media version: plant mom or plant daddy) is one who develops an intuition about what their plant needs without googling its name or its care tips. The difference between killing and caring for any plant should be completely dependent on these three resources. But when you try to grow a plant outside of its natural habitat, the requisite resources double in number. I will use this chapter to introduce and discuss the six individual resources.

☀ Sun
🌡 Temperature
🍽 Nutrients

- ✒ Water
- 🐌 Soil
- ✂ Tools

Plants also need air to survive. They use carbon dioxide (CO_2) from the air to make food and oxygen (O_2) to respire like us. This process is called photosynthesis. On the other hand, respiration is the process where energy is produced from the food that the plants make. While the food is mainly prepared by the green parts of the plant (such as the stem and leaves), respiration is carried out by other parts too, such as the roots. The reason for not including air as a separate resource is threefold. (1) Following the chain of logic, plants basically use air to get macronutrients, which can be covered as part of nutrients. (2) The assumption that your home garden is on planet earth (not in space or a vacuum capsule) is a reasonable one. (3) The motivation behind this book is to simplify, not complicate.

☀ SUN

If you have seen a rainbow or passed sunlight through a prism, you would have noticed that the light splits into seven colour bands. These bands are collectively referred to as VIBGYOR (V for violet, I for indigo, B for blue, G for green, Y for yellow, O for orange and R for red), and each band is connected to a certain wavelength of light. In simple terms, light has different wavelengths, and these wavelengths appear to us in the form of colour bands. All these bands taken together are called a spectrum.

Plants use different parts of this spectrum to grow. While the blue part is responsible for the vegetative growth, i.e., growth of stem and leaves, the red part of the spectrum is known to help in fruiting and flower production.

Man-made light sources that are used in indoor spaces, such as incandescent tube light, fluorescent lights and LED, differ in the intensity of the colour bands as compared to that of the sun spectrum. The intensity of red and blue light is the maximum in sunlight, whereas the intensity of green and blue bands is still closer to man-made lights such as the white LED lights. Therefore, the plants that are grown for their leaves and stem, such as monstera, pothos, peace lily, etc., can be to some extent grown indoors. But plants that we grow for their flowers and fruits, such as daisies, marigolds, lemons, etc., can be grown only near a very well-lit window, outdoors or under a grow light that mimics sunlight's spectrum.

A common symptom to assess if your plant is not getting enough sun is the yellowing of leaves. Plants kept indoors or in dark spaces start losing their green pigment and turn yellow. In this case, try moving it to a brighter space for at least ten days and observe if the new leaves come out healthy or not. Despite the move, if the plant continues to lose colour, then try rectifying the other factors detailed later in this chapter. Since plants cannot speak and communicate their life problems, a good way to understand them is by observing them. They respond to stressful conditions by losing pigment colour and

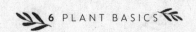

develop droopy leaves and brown edges. Leaf burns can be noticed too.

In overexposed conditions, i.e., when the sun is too intense for the plant, you will again notice yellow leaves, but this time they will show brown burnt spots. In such a scenario, move them to a lesser-lit area. Broadly speaking, by looking at the leaf texture and shape, you can judge if that plant will be 'sun loving' or 'sun hating'. Plants such as aloe vera with waxy coating and thick leaves have evolved to grow in sunny spaces where the sun is directly falling on the plant for at least 4–5 hours, whereas plants such as peace lily that have broad, delicate and thin leaves cannot withstand intense sunlight and prefer filtered light or shade. I am using these examples to communicate the idea of how different plants have different sunlight requirements, but this is not a universal rule. We will talk about the sunlight needs of plants in Parts II and III of this book.

Alternatives: Among the necessary resources, managing sunlight conditions is the hardest. I get it. Buying a house is hard enough but buying one that works for your orchids may be a tall ask. However, you can manipulate the amount of light in your balcony or home with some easy steps.

Dealing With Intense Sunlight Conditions

1. **Use a shade cloth to filter out light.** A common one is a green-coloured fabric made from HDPE (high-

density polyethylene, a kind of plastic) and nylon. This material helps in reducing the intensity of sunlight falling on plants and reduces the evaporation rate from the soil. It is popularly used in greenhouses and plant nurseries. One can install it in a balcony, on a terrace, or in a lawn as well.

2. **Plant arrangement.** If you are looking for something simpler and if you have only a few plants, try using bigger and sun-loving plants on the outskirts of your balcony/window and place the small delicate ones in their shade #Jugaad.

Dealing With Low Sunlight Conditions

1. **Use artificial grow light.** These lights can imitate the sun's spectrum and help the plant grow better in low-light conditions.

2. **Tube lights!** They may also work in certain conditions. Further, tube lights do not heat up on usage. Therefore, you can install them in your plant shelf and keep the plant closest to the light, thereby helping maximize light absorption.

🌡 TEMPERATURE

Most plants can survive in the temperature range of 10–35°C, but where the plant evolved to sustain itself determines the temperature ranges in which it will thrive. To 'thrive' implies conditions that do not stunt a plant's growth in any way. Simply speaking, its stems and leaves are able to grow, flowers are able to bloom

and fruit production is possible. Extremely low or high temperatures can damage plant cells and interfere in its daily processes, thereby hampering plant growth. Obviously, the availability and intensity of sunlight has a direct bearing on temperatures, but their interaction can create different conditions. For example, aloe vera, a succulent evolved to grow in desert-like conditions, enjoys direct sun and high temperatures (above 25°C) while the English rose also likes good sun but thrives in lower temperatures (under 30°C).

I have placed the plants in the forthcoming chapter in three categories.

Low Temperature: Plants that prefer 0–15°C or winter-loving plants. They may survive lower or higher temperatures as well, but key life events such as fruiting, seed germination or flowering will be triggered only in this temperature range.

Medium Temperature: Plants that like 15°C–35°C. These are typical tropical foliage plants that perform their best in terms of vegetative and reproductive growth in this temperature range.

High Temperature: Plants that like 30°C–45°C. These are generally the hydrophobic tropical plants that like high temperatures as they have adapted to arid environments.

To not complicate things, in the chapters on flowering and edible plants, I have categorized areas of our country based on temperature and rainfall as Region 1 and Region 2. Region 1 (including Haryana, Punjab, Rajasthan, Gujarat, Madhya Pradesh, Uttar Pradesh, Bihar, Jharkhand, and West Bengal) experiences spring in February–March, extreme summer during May–July, mild monsoons in July–August, autumn in October and extreme winter in December–January. For Region 2 (including Maharashtra, Karnataka, Kerala, Chattisgarh, Odisha, parts of Tamil Nadu, Andhra Pradesh, Telangana, Assam, Nagaland, and parts of Manipur), I am referring to spring in February–March, mild to extreme summers from May–July, heavy monsoon rains in July–September, mild autumn in October and mild winters in November–January. This classification, I confess, is not the best and does no justice to the geographical diversity of our country, but it should work to convey the idea of what can be grown when. In this classification of Regions 1 and 2, I have not included states, such as Jammu and Kashmir, Ladakh, Meghalaya and parts of Uttarakhand, Himachal and Mizoram, that face extreme weather conditions. Hope it helps.

Finally, but most importantly, home gardeners need to be aware of temperature conditions inside their home or the ambient temperature of the place where they are going to keep a plant. Further, it is important to note that temperature fluctuates within a house. If you have a glass window in your space, then the temperature of the space might actually rise higher than the temperatures outside because glass tends to trap heat, whereas windows with air conditioners installed on them can get very cold when the AC is turned on.

🍴 NUTRIENTS

Plants, like humans, need a regular dose of nutrition. The primary nutrients they need are carbon (C), nitrogen (N), oxygen (O), phosphorus (P) and potassium (K). These nutrients may not be available to the plant in simple forms. Naturally, plants get their dose of nutrition from either soil or air and then break them into simpler forms so that they become usable. Carbon is taken from the air in the form of carbon dioxide during photosynthesis. Plants also take in oxygen from air for energy production, like we humans do, in a process called respiration. What's worth knowing for any home gardener is that plant growth is restricted by macronutrients that come from the soil—N, P and K—which is why most commercial fertilizers are sold as 'NPK'.

Without getting into the complexity of the many chemical processes that these macronutrients are involved in, let me share what their absence typically means for a plant. A nitrogen-deprived plant will fail to achieve full size and may show yellow pale leaves. Inadequate phosphorus makes a plant weak and delays maturity. Potassium deficiency hampers reproduction—

lesser flowers, lesser fruits—and may lead to scorching, curling and/or yellowing leaves.

Apart from macronutrients, plants also need micronutrients, i.e., nutrients that are required in small amounts, like calcium (Ca), manganese (Mn), iron (Fe), boron (B), copper (Cu), zinc (Zn), chlorine (Cl), nickel (Ni), cobalt (Co), sodium (Na) and silicon (Si). However, unlike macronutrients, absence of micronutrients is unlikely to threaten a plant's survival. Therefore, let us limit our attention to macronutrients.

In the natural world, as plants decay and animals poop, nutrients are released into the soil and are taken up by a plant through a phenomenon known as nutrient cycling. But for plants that are grown in pots or in home setups, this natural process of decay and nutrient cycling is not as active. Any existing nutrients in the soil are either taken up by the plant or washed away with water with time. So, we need to regularly replenish the soil by adding more nutrients.

Commercially available sources of nutrients are either 'man-made' inorganic compounds or 'natural' organic compounds. Both are referred to as fertilizers. Man-made fertilizers are processed in a factory or in a lab (urea is an example, used extensively in commercial farming). Natural fertilizers, which I highly recommend for home gardeners, refer to compost or manure. Compost is decayed food waste and manure is decayed cattle poop, both of which are great organic sources of nutrients.

The only advantage that man-made fertilizers offer is ease of nutrient access for plants, as 'pre-processing' ensures that nutrients are available in a form that plants require. When you add factory-made phosphorus or nitrogen to the plant, nutrients that remain unused will still be partly washed away. Why? Because plants cannot take up nutrients all at once. Nutrients in natural fertilizers, such as compost or manure, don't have the same problem. Natural fertilizers require insects and microbes (tiny organisms that you can't see with naked eyes) to break these nutrients into simple forms for plant intake. This process is slow, but it's a sustainable way to fertilize your plants. An added advantage is that some of these insects also help with soil aeration and drainage, which basically makes your soil healthier.

The frequency of addition of these nutrient supplements depends on the kind of plants you are growing. For home gardening, I can think of three kinds of nutrient feeders.

Heavy Feeders
These are plants that need a lot of nutrients and good quality fertilizer but may differ in terms of frequency with regard to fertilization needs. I have further divided them into two categories:

Regular Heavy Feeders
The kind that grow quickly, attaining their full size in a few months and needing fertilizer monthly. Common example: most vegetables.

Seasonal Heavy Feeders

These are plants that attain their maximum vegetative growth, i.e., stem and root growth, in a few years but flower and fruit only in a certain season. For such plants, add fertilizer when you start seeing flowers on them, and if you already know about when this plant flowers, then preferably add fertilizer before the flowering season. The idea is to supplement the plant with nutrients before it gets burdened with the reproductive growth pressure (in the form of flowers and fruits). This will help improve flowering and fruiting. For such plants, use superior quality compost or manure because if the plant doesn't get enough nutrients, the blooming will be compromised and you will have to wait for the next flowering season, which might be only once a year. Common example: most fruiting trees.

Medium Feeders

Think of these as plants that show a few inches of growth per season (~three months). They would need to be fertilized at least once every season. Common example: most foliage plants.

Rare Feeders

Plants that can sustain well in low nutrient conditions. These are plants that grow only a few centimetres per season. You can even add old compost for such plants once a year. Given their low nutrient requirement, using fresh compost will be a waste of resources. Common example: most succulents.

✎ WATER

Water has three primary functions for a plant: 1) It carries nutrients from one part of the plant to another while moving through tubes called xylem. 2) It is a key component in several chemical reactions, photosynthesis being one of the most important ones. 3) It is responsible for temperature regulation in the plant. Water evaporation through small holes called stomata helps in temperature regulation.

The challenge is to hit the right balance, which is why when you complain of yellowing leaves, any plant doctor would first ask you to look for watering problems. In the absence of water, all plant cells will shrink and lose their ability to carry out their functions. On the other hand, overwatering will lead to water-clogged air pockets, limiting oxygen availability for plant roots. Prolonged exposure to any kind of water stress, over- or underwatering can cause yellowing of plant leaves and eventual death. Generally, underwatering plants show brown edges, yellow and paper-dry leaves, while overwatered plants not only have yellow leaves, but the leaves also seem mushy on touching. Every plant has different water requirements: some plants like moist soil, others prefer dry soil. For example, snake plant (a succulent) prefers dry soil, so even if you've forgotten to water this plant for a month, it will most likely not die. However, an aglaonema, a large-leaf delicate plant, will definitely die if not watered for a month since it has not evolved to endure long dry spells. I cannot tell you the exact days for watering because the microenvironment for every home varies. However, the plants covered in this book are largely classified into three watering categories:

Occasional Watering

Plants classified as xerophytes have adapted to grow in low-water conditions such as deserts and snow-covered regions. You can try watering such plants once every fifteen days, but I will let you in on my secret: get a small potted aloe vera plant (or any plant under five inches in leaf length) and be prepared to let it die. It won't. Here's what you need to do.

> Step 1: Do not water the plant for five days.
> Step 2: Gently pull out the plant from the pot along with the soil. Turning the pot upside down will help.
> Step 3: Touch the bottom-most soil and see if it feels sticky.
> Step 4: Put the plant back the way it was.

Now on to the analysis. If the soil at the bottom doesn't feel sticky, you would know that the fifth day is a great day to water such a plant. If the bottom soil feels sticky, however, repeat steps 2-4 every alternate day. When it stops feeling sticky, that is the number of days it takes for soil to completely dry in your place. The reason I suggested aloe vera for this learning experiment is because it is a hardy plant and this regular pulling out will not kill it. Nobody is born with a green thumb; it takes time to learn and experiment with plants and help them grow better.

Medium Watering

These are plants that neither love water, nor hate it. For such plants, let the topsoil dry between waterings. One way to check this is by poking your finger an inch deep and noting when you get soil sticking to your hand. This method may not be the most scientific approach to watering, but it is great to keep medium-watering plants alive. You can also invest in a moisture assessment metre, but for beginners, it's not worth the investment. So, you add water for such plants when the topsoil is dry and is not sticking to your finger.

Wet Feet

I feel that plants that like wet feet are tricky because they like moist soil, but not water-saturated soil. I will try and avoid such plants as I wish to encourage you to start gardening and not be scared of it. However, generally, plants that like moist soil are the ones that like regular daily watering and well-draining soil so that the water does not occupy all the air pockets.

Regardless of the category the plant falls in, there are two things that are commonly applicable to all plants. I call these my watering techniques.

1. **Always water your plants thoroughly.** The differentiation in the above classifications should be the frequency of watering, not the amount. Often people forget to thoroughly water their plants, meaning that they will only moisten the top layer of the soil, which leaves the lower section of the roots water-deprived. This uneven distribution of water

through the root system can put the plant in stress. If you are worried that thorough watering of the plant might lead to a dirty floor, you can use drainage plates under pots to collect excess water.

2. **Invest in a watering can/hose.** The best way for any home gardener to water plants is to use a watering can or a watering hose. The idea is to use something that helps to reduce the water pressure as it falls on the delicate parts of the plant, especially if it is a young plant or one with delicate leaves.

SOIL

Soil is essentially a solid matrix that holds nutrients and water for the plant, helping it to grow. So, the perfect soil is one that has all the relevant nutrients to support plant growth and provide the apt amount of moisture for it. Regular soil that you find in your backyard may be perfect or could be made perfect with some help. This 'help' could be in the form of additional nutrients, water drainage or retention. However, before we get there, as with previous resources, let's start by classifying soil types and understanding their properties. I find it most useful to do so on the basis of its colour (applicable for the Indian subcontinent).

Types of Soil

Reddish Brown Soil: Rich in iron.

Commonly Found In: Kerala, Tamil Nadu, Madhya Pradesh, Goa, Andhra Pradesh, Karnataka, Assam and parts of Odisha

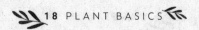

Water Drainage: Medium

Nutrient Level: Low

This soil is also known as laterite soil.

Grey Soil: Deprived in organic matter and key minerals.

Commonly Found In: Punjab, Haryana, Delhi, Uttar Pradesh

Water Drainage: Medium

Nutrient Level: Low

This type of soil is also referred to as alluvial soil.

> #FUNFACT: *How was alluvial soil formed?*
> *Our earth is made of large rock plates called tectonic plates. These plates keep moving very slowly in different directions. About 40–50 million years ago, when a plate known as the Indian plate started moving towards the Eurasian plate, the sea between these two plates drained out into the ocean now known as the Indian Ocean. The solid bottom of that sea started rising up under the pressure of the Indian plate pushing against the Eurasian plate. This rising sea bottom is now*

known as the Himalayas. The sea that was drained out left behind silt which today forms the grey-coloured alluvial soil that is found in north Indian states. And did you know that the Himalayas are still rising in height? Yes, they are—by 1 cm each year.

Black Soil: Rich in clay, organic matter, iron and aluminium compounds.

Commonly Found In: Maharashtra, Madhya Pradesh, Tamil Nadu, parts of Gujarat and Andhra Pradesh

Water Drainage: Low

Nutrient Level: High

Red and Yellow Soil: Contains a mixture of iron and metamorphic rocks.

Commonly Found In: Areas along the Western Ghats, Odisha and Chhattisgarh

Water Drainage: High

Nutrient Level: High

At this point, I would recommend that you step outside your house, go to a park and look closely at the soil.

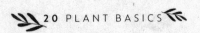

Chances are you won't find perfectly yellow, grey or black soil. It will probably be a mixture. Try digging out a handful of soil with anything sharp or with your hands. Bring that home, moisten the soil with plain water (do not drench the soil, just moisten it). (see illustration below for these steps). Now try making a ball out of it with your hands. If it's difficult to make a perfect ball and it keeps breaking, then the sand content is higher than the other contents of soil such as silt and clay. However, if you can make a perfect ball, that means your soil is clayey or silty. Then, further roll this ball into a snake-like shape. If you can roll out a snake-like shape without any cracks, your soil is high in clay, but if it breaks in between, then the silt content is higher.

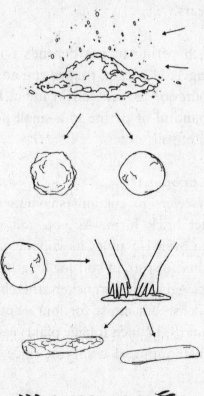

The purpose of this 'back-to-childhood-days' exercise is to help you understand the drainage and nutrient status of the soil near you. Depending on what soil you find in your area, here is what you can do to improve it:

For Better Drainage

If the water often stands above the soil in your pots, it's a sign that the soil needs better drainage.

a. Add Perlite

Perlite is a white amorphous substance that comes out of volcanic eruptions. Chemically speaking, its structure is similar to that of glass. It is a low-density material that will help retain air pockets in soil for several years.

How much perlite to use depends on the kind of soil you have. However, to give you an idea, for any regular outdoor garden soil in India, I recommend using a handful of perlite in a small pot (5–6-inch-deep pot) of soil.

b. Add Cocopeat

Cocopeat refers to coconut shavings that come in a compact brick form. As you add water, it can expand to over 4–5 times its volume. Cocopeat will help retain moisture in soil for long periods of time without clogging the air pockets, thereby keeping the soil less dense but moist for long. You can grow a small plant (8–12-inch foliage plant) just in cocopeat with regular input of compost, since the cocopeat

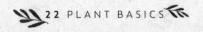

will act as a substrate to hold plant roots and the compost will act as a nutrient source.

c. Add River Sand
Mix river sand with clayey soil in a 1:3 proportion. Avoid using beach sand because it contains high amounts of salts that poison some plant roots.

For making the soil nutrient-rich or to help with faster plant growth, here is what you can add.

a. Compost/Vermicompost
Fertilizer prepared from food material primarily digested by microbes is called compost, and the one digested by microbes as well as worms, such as earthworms, is called vermicompost. Although both of them are great sources of all macronutrients, vermicompost is known to be slightly richer in nutrients than compost.

b. Manure
Fertilizer prepared from cattle dung digested over time in the open is referred to as manure. Some shops also sell fresh dung, but I recommend using the decayed form because research shows that the decayed form of dung (as manure) supports better growth in plants. Additionally, manure has no foul smell unlike fresh cattle dung.

Please note that fresh manure and compost have low pH, meaning they are slightly acidic. It is important

to not add fresh compost/manure immediately to the plants because not all plants can tolerate acidic soil. Allowing manure/compost to dry in the air for 2–3 days aids in increasing the pH towards neutral. Further, this helps in getting rid of unwanted insects such as spiders, beetles and worms. One can try sieving the dried compost/manure through a metal sieve with a mesh size of approximately 1–3 cm.

If all the above details on soil are confusing or too much to take in, here's a recipe for two soil mixes that any home gardener can use for most needs.

a. Regular Soil Mix
Use equal amounts of compost (for nutrition), cocopeat (for low density and moisture retainment) and regular outdoor soil (for root support).

b. Succulent Soil Mix*
Use river sand or perlite (for good drainage), old compost (because plants where this soil will be used don't need many nutrients) and regular outdoor soil (for root support) in equal quantities.

⚡ TOOLS
So far, I have introduced you to what's necessary for any plant. This section is dedicated to explaining the basic tools that any home gardener would need or should be aware of. Technically, a plant won't die without them, but these tools are important for many reasons, ranging

---

* You can also purchase premixed soil from a nursery or online. They work fine too.

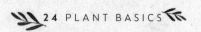

from a gardener's safety to the healthy upkeep of plants. Admittedly, I cannot cover the entire universe of tools (and their avatars), but I have tried to write this section as a glossary, keeping in mind the most common queries I receive about gardening tools on my social media handles.

1. Pots and Grow Bags

You need something to contain soil. That's where pots come in. In the market, there are currently various options available in which to grow plants. Here's a brief on what I think about these pots.

a. Terracotta Pots

Functionally superior and environment friendly, but short lifespan.

Terracotta pots are my favourite for two reasons. First, during extreme hot summers, the soil in terracotta pots is able to retain moisture for long, and the temperature in such pots remains lower than their closest competition, the plastic pots. Second, a terracotta pot is baked soil that can be painted every Diwali or every year, and, if it breaks, it will eventually erode to become soil.

b. Concrete Pots

Functionally superior with long lifespan, but very heavy.

Concrete pots can last a little longer than a terracotta pot but are very heavy. They are a feasible option for growing plants for people who stay in self-owned homes, but not for people who stay in rental homes because moving them around can be really difficult. Just like terracotta pots, they can protect the soil from getting extremely hot during summers and also reduce the rate of evaporation, thereby helping to keep the soil moist for longer in dry seasons.

c. Plastic pots
Long lifespan and easy to move, but environmentally unfriendly.

Plastic pots are lighter in weight compared to concrete or terracotta pots. For gardeners staying in highrises and rental apartments, they are a more feasible option, especially for growing large plants. However, there are two problems with plastic pots. Apart from being an environmental problem, plastic also gets heated up fairly quickly, especially if you stay in a region that has extremely hot summers.

d. Ceramic Pots
Long lifespan and beautiful, but heavy and expensive. I recommend ceramic pots for decorative purposes. They might be heavy, they might be expensive, but the charm we can add to any space indoors with the plant is exceptional. I would personally suggest using ceramic pots for decorative purposes mostly inside your home. If the ceramic pot has a drainage hole at the bottom, you can directly start a plant in it but if it doesn't, you'll have to use a second pot (with holes at the bottom) and then keep that in the ceramic pot.

e. Metal Pots
Beautiful, but corrode quickly.

Metal pots are decorative pieces that you can use to grow plants. The only problem is that due to continuous exposure to water, they may start corroding. My quick tip for using metal pots would be to first plant them in a plastic pot and then keep that inside the metal pot. This will reduce the exposure to water and enhance the life of the metal pot. They look great as hanging metal trays for balconies and railings.

f. Grow Bags
Easy to use and cheap, but these get dirty underneath.

Currently, there are three kinds of grow bags in the market: one is just a plastic sleeve (which can contain the soil to grow plants), the second is an HDPE plastic grow bag (which is a thicker version of plastic sleeves and has a longer lifespan than the regular plastic sleeve) and the third is a fabric grow bag. My personal choice is a geo fabric grow bag for two reasons. First, they can hold the structure better than any other kind of grow bags, and second, they are essentially recycled plastic which is mixed with some fabric material, thereby making them environmentally friendly.

A common problem with any pot is that as the water drains out from the drainage holes over time, it makes the concrete or the tiled floor dirty. Therefore, I recommend using a drainage plate under any kind of pot that has a drainage hole at the bottom.

Alternative: If you want to start gardening today and do not want to wait to buy a pot, you will find an alternative in your house. Essentially, anything that can hold soil with a few drainage holes at the bottom will do the job. The size depends on the plant, but right from an old bucket, a PET bottle, a kitchen *matka*, a paint drum, a broken coffee mug, food-delivery containers—anything can be used to grow plants. Just ensure that you make a couple of holes at the bottom to allow water to seep out. If the holes are too big, use gravel at the base of the pot to block these holes.

Pot Size

You may use any style or shape of a pot for growing any plant, but one thing your plant won't be able to ignore is the size of the pot. Size is essentially a proxy for how much nutrients and space will be available for the plant to grow. As the plant reaches new heights, the demand for nutrients and space increases. While the need for nutrients can be catered to by regular supplementation with fertilizer, there is no other way to give more space for the roots. Large trees that you might have observed on roadsides sometimes also uproot the entire pavement with their roots. When there is not enough space for the roots to grow in the soil, the plant will start looking for whatever little space it gets. Next to a charcoaled road under the brick-paved walkway, there might be a network of roots ten metres deep or more, and the pavement might be limiting the tree's growth.

When you plant a plant in the ground directly, there are options for it to grow vertically and sideways, but when you grow plants in a pot, space becomes a limitation. As a general rule of thumb, what I recommend for gardeners is to increase the size of the pot in proportion to the size of the plants. However, this relationship is not strictly linear. The method I will share with you is not very scientific but works for home gardeners.

For a <2 feet plant, get a 5–6 inch pot
For a 2–4 feet plant, get a 10–12 inch pot
For a 4–6 feet plant, get a 20–22 inch pot
For a 6–8 feet plant, get a 26–28 inch pot

For anything larger than 8–10 feet, I recommend growing in soil directly because a pot to support such a huge plant will weigh over several kilograms and moving them around would literally need a mini crane. In such a case, it's better to move the plant in the ground directly.

Most pots you get in the market are described by their depth. So, an 8-inch pot means a pot with a depth of eight inches, and the diameter will be in proportion to the depth. Also, remember that the plant roots grow both vertically and sideways in the pot, searching not only for nutrients but also for a better grip on soil to support the plant's weight above ground.

Apart from leafy and tuberous vegetables, I recommend growing only one plant per pot. Otherwise, the two plants growing together will start competing with each other for resources and end up not growing to their full potential.

2. Pruners and Trimmers

Pruning and trimming means selective removal of parts of the plant, both dead or living, such as branches, stems, buds, flowers, etc. This is important in order to promote the growth and flowering of a plant. Depending on what part of the plant you need to prune and how much power and sharpness that part would require for pruning, you can determine the tool of your choice. There is a whole range of pruners available in the market. Some basic ones useful for a home gardener are as follows:

a. Hand Shear

They can be used to cut any kind of twig or branch, alive or dead, that is up to a thickness of half an inch. It has two blades that can be used for pruning any kind of shrub, such as rose stems, hydrangea stems, etc.

b. Loppers

They are very similar to a hand shear, the only difference being that the blades of a lopper are thicker and the handles are bigger, making them easier to use for a thicker branch/stem (up to 2–3 inches in diameter). They are worth buying if you have a lemon or a banana plant at home.

c. Anvil Pruner

They function like a scissor and are used for removing dead wood. Although their grip is good, they don't give a clean cut.

d. Bypass Pruner

One blade bypasses the counterblade, giving a clean cut and thereby making it suitable for pruning those parts of the plant which are green and alive. They are not suitable for cutting dead wood.

Alternative: A good sturdy pair of scissors with a comfortable grip can be used for all minor pruning purposes. However, the only limitation is that when we use scissors for cutting thick stems, the blades will spread and not cut through cleanly. In that case, a sharp knife can be used, although one must be careful while using them and preferably wear gloves to protect their fingers. If you have a bunch of plants, getting a good bypass pruner will be a great investment for you.

Other Tools You May Need

For absolute beginner-level gardeners, I recommend investing in a good watering can. They are available in two materials: plastic and metal. I prefer the latter because of their look as they come in a wide range of colours. While buying a watering can, ensure that either it has a long nose or there is a nozzle at the end that spreads water as a fountain.

For gardeners who have graduated from two or three plants to ten or more, investing in gardening gloves would be helpful. They will help protect your hands from prickly plants and keep them clean when you repot your plants. Soil also contains small ticks that are difficult to see with the naked eye, but these insects can bite and cause skin irritation. For such cases, gloves will come in handy as a precaution.

Irrespective of their level, a gardener must have a spraying bottle. A one-litre bottle is good. It will come in handy for any kind of treatment where you have to spray the insecticide/pesticide/neem oil.

Apart from the above, I have not invested my money in anything else as a home gardener. In fact, when I started keeping plants, all I had was a plastic bottle which I used as a watering can, and a pair of scissors. My toolkit has evolved over time, but I still reach out mostly for just the watering can and a good pruner.

Key Takeaways
- What a plant needs depends on the habitat it has evolved to grow in.
- You can manipulate the sun availability, temperature, humidity and soil type to mimic the habitat suitable for plant growth.
- If you are a complete beginner at gardening, invest in good-quality tools that will protect you and help care for your plants better.

Chapter 2

THIRTEEN COMMON 'HOW TOS'

In your journey of gardening, here are some quick 'how tos' that will come in handy.

1. HOW TO REPOT A PLANT

When a plant is root-bound, there is no more space for the roots to grow and they start peeping out from the bottom drainage hole, it is a good time to move the plant to a bigger pot. If you see the roots growing out from the base of the pot, you can be sure that the plant is root-bound.

Further, when you buy a plant from the garden centre that comes in a plastic sleeve, you can transfer the plant to a new pot.

Here is how to go about it.

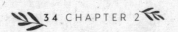

a. Stop watering the plant for 2–3 days, allowing the soil to dry. This will reduce the chances of hurting the roots when you pull out the plant later.

b. On the second or third day, gently pull out the plant while giving support to the main stem at the same time. If need be, you can turn the pot upside down and give it a slight nudge at the base of the pot. Repotting should be done during the evening so that the plant is not exposed to the sun (read: heat stress) immediately.

c. In case you notice that the roots are overgrown/root-bound, try loosening them gently, otherwise avoid disturbing the root ball. For a healthy repotting, keeping the main root undisturbed is the key.

d. The new pot where you wish to transfer the plant should be 2–3 inches bigger than the current pot.

e. Fill the lower one-third of the new pot with soil, gently pressing it to block the drainage holes. This will allow only water to escape and not the soil.

f. Now place the plant in the pot and fill the empty space with soil, keeping the top one inch vacant for water to sit whenever you water the plant.

g. For repotting, it is important to place the plant in the shade for at least a day or two, so that in case you happened to disturb a few roots, the shade will keep it cool and comfy for the plant to recover from the shock.

At times, a plant may take longer to recover. If your plant continues to dry and droop, don't be disheartened. You can try practicing repotting with a different plant again. The key is to loosen the roots in order to break their root memory while keeping the root system intact so that they can quickly settle in a new pot.

2. HOW TO GET RID OF INSECTS

Primarily, there are two kinds of troublemakers in a home garden: insects and fungus.

Insects may be eating your plants (e.g., caterpillars, beetles), sucking on your plants (e.g., mealybugs), colonizing your plants to lay eggs (e.g., whiteflies), or just crawling in the soil (e.g., nematodes). To get rid of any of the above, you can use various neem derivatives.

For infected plant parts above the soil, spray a mixture of 10 ml of neem oil in a litre of water with 3–5 drops of liquid soap (soap will help the oil to bind with water).

For infected soil, mix 200–300 grams of neem cake or neem powder in the top 2-inch soil layer. The chemicals in neem interfere in the hormonal system of insects and hamper their growing and laying of eggs. The abovementioned dosage of neem is recommended for a medium-sized pot (10–12 inch deep). You can scale to proportion accordingly for bigger or smaller pots or follow the instructions on the product label.

Please note that not all insects are bad. Ladybugs, mantises and bees are a few of the good ones which you would need in your garden and which contribute to the good health of plants.

3. HOW TO WATER A PLANT

Different plants may have different water needs, but there is only one correct way of watering them: thoroughly!

Add water to the soil, ensuring that the pressure is not so much that the roots of the plant get exposed. Keep watering until it starts coming out from the base of the pot. While watering, you can also practice watering the soil evenly. Such thorough and even watering ensures that the entire root system gets water. Shallow watering reaches only the top set of roots, keeping the bottom roots thirsty. This uneven watering can lead to the slow deterioration of the root system, eventually stunting the growth of the plant.

You can also find people spraying water on the plant. This practice can help to increase the ambient humidity, reduce the ambient temperature or even clean the leaves, but for a plant to absorb water, you will have to add water to the soil directly so that the roots can transfer that water to the various plant parts.

For watering, I recommend using a watering can with the nozzle or a watering hose with a sprayer at the end. If you are using a mug or a bucket, do not water from a height as it displaces soil, thereby exposing the plant roots and causing hurt to delicate plant parts. You can also try placing your fingers in between to reduce the pressure of falling water from a bucket or a mug.

Alternatively, you can also make a DIY watering can. Take a 2–4 litre plastic bottle with its cap. Make 4–8 holes on the cap and use the bottle as a watering can.

Now, if you are wondering what the right time to water your plants is, I would suggest early morning. During the daytime, especially in the afternoon when the sun is intense, the temperature is at its highest and, consequently, the rate of evaporation for the plant (loss of water) is also at its peak. Watering in the mornings will help your plant fight water stress. In case you water in the evening, your plant will be standing with wet feet (clogged soil pockets for roots) over the entire night when the water stress is the lowest.

Therefore, watering before the sun gets over your head is a good practice. However, having said that, my personal recommendation is that whenever you remember to water your plants, just water them. There is no evidence suggesting that a certain timing of watering helps plants grow better for home gardens. Water whenever you can!

4. HOW TO PROPAGATE A PLANT

Propagation technically means growing a new plant, which can be done through a seed or even from a part of the parent plant. Here are some common ways you would need to know for propagation of your plant.

a. How to Propagate a Plant From a Cutting

Cutting means a section of a plant that you can take to grow more plant babies. The most common way of doing that is by looking for a node on your plant. The node is that part of the stem where a stem is dividing into another stem or branch. Take a cutting by chopping just underneath the node. Ensure that you have 3–5 leaves on the cutting. The point from where you take a cutting has the ability to grow a callus or tiny roots. Once the cutting develops roots, it can be potted in soil or allowed to continue in water.

Plants like golden pothos, most kinds of philodendrons, monstera, lucky bamboo, and mint can very easily grow roots on the cutting when kept in water for a week or more. Thus, growing them from a cutting is the most convenient way instead of growing them from a seed.

To improve your success with cuttings, try and take multiple quantities of them. For example, to grow one cutting, I start with at least three. If done right, all three of them may root. However, sometimes only one or two may root. There are two stages where I have seen people go wrong with the stem-cutting propagation.

- *The cutting might turn yellow and dry without developing roots.*
  In such a case, in your next attempt, first ensure that you make the cut below the node because this point releases growth hormones that help in root growth. Further, always choose a healthy-looking stem to take a cutting. If you see any kinds of marks or spots on the stem, avoid using that one to take a cutting.

- *The cutting develops roots but fails to establish itself in the soil and dies quickly.*

  This happens when the cutting undergoes shock and fails to sustain that shock. When you move a cutting from water to soil, life can be difficult for that cutting because water is not that easily available for the plant to absorb anymore. To improve your success rate with a cutting, keep it in a shaded space for a couple of days when you pot it so that it is not exposed to the sun. This will reduce the wilting that intense sunlight causes in a newly potted cutting and give time for the cutting to establish deeper roots.

In the chapters to follow, I will refer to this propagation method as the 'stem-cutting' method.

b. How to Use Rooting Hormone

Some plants that can be propagated using cuttings sometimes need a little extra help to develop roots. This extra help can be provided in the form of a synthetic rooting hormone, which is a chemical powder that protects the cutting from rotting (developing fungus) when placed in soil.

The process of taking the cutting remains the same: just dip the fresh exposed part of the stem in rooting hormone and place it in the soil directly in a 4–5-inch pot. Water the soil whenever the top layer feels dry upon touching. In 7–14 days, the cutting should develop roots. You can continue in this pot or move the cutting to a bigger pot. Plants with hardy or wooden stems, such as fiddle-leaf fig and rubber plant, propagate well with rooting hormone.

Instead of the synthetic chemical, you can also use an organic substitute—honey. Antimicrobial properties of honey help the plant develop callus without fungal decay in the same way as the synthetic rooting hormone. However, in my experience, the success rate with honey has been relatively much lower as compared to rooting hormone. If you have a bunch of plants to be propagated, I would recommend investing in a small 50–100-gram box of commercial rooting hormone powder.

In the chapters to follow, I will call this propagation method 'cutting with rooting hormone'.

c. How to Divide and Propagate

In a mature plant of banana, aloe vera or alocasia, you can spot a bunch of the younger versions of the plant growing alongside the main plant. These young ones are lateral shoots coming out of the soil. If any of them are growing in a pot, pull out the entire plant, holding it at the base of the stem, along with the soil. Look for small shoots that have healthy leaves as well as roots. Separate such shoots (or pups) and pot them in a new pot (4–5 inches deep). If the plant is growing in the ground, you will have to dig around the pup to separate it from the mother plant.

In the chapters to follow, I will refer to this propagation method as the 'divide and grow' method.

d. How to Start a Plant From a Seed

Seeds can be germinated in soil, tissue paper or even in expandable cocopeat balls. They essentially need a substrate that can provide support for the roots to grow and moisture for the seeds to sprout. When the seed opens up and sends out cotyledons (the first set of leaves), they do not require an external source of nutrients since the seed itself is able to provide the nutrients for them. Therefore, for germination, you can use any of the abovementioned substrates. Seeds that germinate easily (e.g., spinach) do not need to be put in a tissue paper or any kind of a starter ball or seedling substrate. You can directly put them in soil. For seeds that need some sort of preconditioning to open up (e.g., chillies, lentils, capsicum), use the tissue-paper method. Place a couple of seeds in a tissue paper and cover it with two more layers of tissue paper. Spray just enough water to keep it moist but not soaked in water. Now place them in a poly bag or a zip-lock bag and try to seal it so that minimum water escapes from the bag. Place this in a sunny spot or a place that will keep it warm for the seeds to germinate faster. As the cotyledons sprout out from the seed, you can take this 'seedling' carefully out from the tissue paper and plant it in a 2–3-inch pot in soil.

In the chapters to follow, I will refer to this propagation method as the 'seed germination' method.

5. HOW TO INCREASE HUMIDITY FOR PLANTS

Plants like calatheas, caladiums and aglaonema appreciate high humidity (approximately 75%). There are two ways to artificially make a space more humid:

a. Invest in an ultrasonic humidifier, a machine that dispenses vapours of water into the air. They are compact and small machines that barely make any sound. Humidifiers come with a range of water storage tank sizes ranging from 300 ml to a couple of litres.

b. If you have only a few plants, you can also use a DIY-humidifier. Take a drainage plate filled with gravel and add water to it. Keep your plant on top of this gravel and fill water as it dries up in the plate. This method works very well for plants such as maidenhair fern. As the water evaporates, it will make the immediate space around the plant cool and humid.

c. You can also use a large plastic box as a greenhouse that helps in reducing water loss. Choose a box with a lid, fill the base with half an inch of water and place the pots with seedlings inside this box. This is super helpful in improving germination.

6. HOW TO MAINTAIN SOIL IN POTS FOR LONG

As the soil gets 'old' in the pot with a plant growing in it, two things happen. First, the soil loses nutrients as they are taken up by the plant or washed away with water. Second, the soil becomes more compact with reduced air cavities. Here are two steps you can follow to 'freshen up' the soil:

a. Stop watering the soil for a day or two. Pull the plant out as you would do for repotting. Gently try loosening the soil from the roots to break root memory.

b. Mix equal amounts of perlite (not compulsory), cocopeat and compost. Use this potting mix to layer the base of the pot, place the plant back and fill the empty space with the new potting mix.

By doing so, you have added a new source of nutrients (compost) for the plant, cocopeat and perlite to keep the soil lightweight and create air pockets for new roots to breathe and grow. A plant needs this kind of repotting only once in 2–3 years. If you continue repotting your plant as it grows out of its pot, you wouldn't need to do anything new for it.

7. HOW TO GROW MICROGREENS

In the section on edibles, I cover mostly herbs, vegetables and fruits. However, in the last decade or so, a new concept of food growing that has emerged is 'microgreens'. Originally, it was reported that microgreens had first been sighted in the state of California in the United States of America in the 1980s. In India, however, it is only in the past few years that you may have noticed a tray of tiny greens growing on restaurant countertops, especially in high-end hotels and airport lounges. The reason for their popularity is partly the hint of freshness and taste they add to food and partly for their nutrient content.

a. What are Microgreens?

Microgreens refer to the first stage of seed germination when you see 2–4 leaves sprouting out of the seed. One can harvest these leaves along with the stem and use them uncooked in salads and sandwiches.

b. Which Seeds to Use?

Microgreens can be grown for mustard, beetroot, carrots, radish, amaranth, sunflower, fenugreek, green moong dal, rajma beans, spinach, broccoli and kale, to name a few. A precautionary advice: not all kinds of plants growing from seeds can be grown as microgreens. Some edible plants like potatoes actually have toxic leaves. So, a quick search on the internet for confirmation is advisable.

For the plant list mentioned above, you can buy the regular seeds (used for growing the actual plant) for microgreens as well.

c. Steps to Grow Microgreens

- Take a 2–3-inch-deep plastic pot/container with a few drainage holes at the bottom and fill it with regular garden soil. Instead of soil, you can also use moistened cocopeat.
- Spread the seeds on the soil in any fashion (at least 1 cm apart) and cover with half an inch of soil.

- Add water, ensuring that the seeds are not exposed, until it starts running out from the base.
- Place the container in a spot which receives 2–3 hours of direct sunlight. You can also cover the container with a lid to reduce moisture loss. Otherwise, add water every time the top layer of soil looks dried up.
- Depending on the kind of seed, you should see the plant cotyledon emerging in 5–10 days. Let them grow for another 2–3 days and harvest using a pair of scissors.

You can store microgreens in a refrigerator inside a steel box lined with tissue paper and use as a topping for any dish that you wish to make more interesting. They can also be fed to children as a nutrition-rich dose of greens.

8. HOW TO PREPARE COMPOST AT HOME

Compost is decayed kitchen waste that can be a great nutrition source for plants. You can start composting at home in a couple of simple steps.

a. Things You Would Need

Nutrient source: Food waste (>250 grams) (except for bones, meat pieces, fish parts, lemons and chillies) and dried leaves (the proportion of food to dried leaves should be 1:2).

Microbial source: A glass (250 ml) of buttermilk/ handful of garden soil, bokashi powder (important when you don't have access to dried leaves)

Container: Composting bin/terracotta khamba/large terracotta matka

Space: Preferably a warm space with ventilation

b. Steps to be Followed

Step 1: Collect kitchen waste every day and start dumping it in a terracotta pot that has a few holes at the bottom or use a khamba (see illustration).

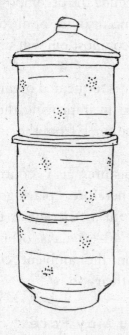

Step 2: Mix the kitchen waste with buttermilk and soil.

Step 3: Line the mixture with 1–2-inch layer of dried leaves. If you don't have access to leaves, use bokashi powder.

Repeat steps 1–3 every time you have to add kitchen waste. You can do this once a day or even once a week, depending on the waste output from your kitchen. Buttermilk and soil can be skipped once you have started the composting process.

c. Science Behind Composting

Your food waste is a rich source of nitrogen that is balanced by the carbon from the dried leaves. Microbes performing the decomposition of food waste will need a balanced source of nitrogen and carbon as otherwise your compost bin will start smelling.

Bokashi powder is fermented organic matter that can be super helpful in improving the composting rate and reducing the smell from the bin.

Heat and moisture also contribute to speedy composting. Therefore, placing the khamba or composting bin in a balcony or terrace helps. The compost takes 40–60 days or more to be ready depending upon the ambient conditions for the microbes to do their job.

d. Issues You May Face

Insects: Spotting spiders, lizards, beetles and worms is completely normal in a compost bin. They are all helping in the process of composting. In fact, imagine your compost bin as a mini ecosystem where all the flora and fauna play a key role in the sustenance of life. However, if problematic insects such as ants start flourishing in the bin, use a concentrated neem-based repellent spray around the bin.

Foul smell: The carbon to nitrogen ratio needs to be right in order to balance and counteract the smell. Use dried leaves or bokashi powder for this purpose. Additionally, aerate the mixture every 20–30 days in order to introduce more oxygen for microbial decomposition.

Slow decomposition: Eliminate the factors such as moisture and microbial source to figure out what is delaying the decomposition. Start with ensuring that there is enough soil and buttermilk to initiate microbial growth, then see if the bin is placed in an area with a temperature of at least 25°C or higher.

Further, the mixture in the bin should neither look watery nor completely dry as otherwise the microbes will not do their job efficiently. You can manipulate the moisture either by adding water or by adding dried water-absorbing substrates like sawdust and dried leaves. Some people may recommend cardboard or newspaper pieces, but I have found them to decompose much slower than food.

Tip: I add two large handfuls of cocopeat and cow dung balls per 20-litre pot of compost bin to improve its nutrient content. You can also mix ground eggshell in the compost bin to make it phosphorus-rich, something that works wonders in flowering plants.

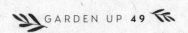

e. Why You Should Compost

Firstly, when you start separating the kitchen food waste from the rest of the waste going out of your house, you are significantly reducing the burden on the landfills. These are large mounds of waste that are situated outside every big city/town of our country.

Secondly, you become self-reliant for fertilizer production needed for growing your own food, flowers or ornamental plants.

9. HOW TO GROW A BONSAI TREE

Growing a small tree in a container by maintaining the shape and scale of that of a full-sized tree is called Bonsai. It is a very popular artform practiced in Japan, and it is believed to have originated first in the Chinese Empire. One does not need genetically dwarfed tree seeds but rather a lot of patience to make a bonsai.

a. Starting a Bonsai

You can start from a seed, but it can take a very long time to have a sizable bonsai. Therefore, sourcing from a mature plant works out better. Depending on the plant type and accessibility, bonsai artists generally use a cutting from an older plant. For home gardeners such as myself, buying a prepared bonsai and then shaping it further is more practical than starting from scratch. If you wish to start from a cutting, use the air layering method (this is discussed in the chapter on 'how to grow edibles').

b. Requirements

Pot: The size of the pot depends on the size of the bonsai you are starting with. It should be big enough to accommodate the soil covering the roots for moisture but, at the same time, small enough for restricting the plant growth.

Soil: The soil should have good drainage properties in order to avoid root rot.

Drainage aid: You can use small crushed coal pieces or some gravel.

Accessories: Moss can be added to accessorize your bonsai.

c. Method

- If you are going to use a small tree already in a bonsai state, or a rooted tree branch or a new plant that you want to shape into a bonsai, prune it into the desired shape and leave for 2–3 days to recover from the open cuts.
- Take the plant out of the original pot and try getting rid of the soil sticking to the roots. Sometimes the roots may be highly entangled, in which case you can clean them with a brush and remove as much dirt as possible from them. If the brush does not work very efficiently, then you can also use a water spray and wash away the small lumps of soil.

- Once the roots are clean or you have a clear visual of them, prune the root branches to adjust them in a new bonsai pot.
- Pruning the roots to the right size is important. If they are too big, they quickly run out of the bonsai pot, but if they are too small, they might not be able to sustain the water requirements of the plant. The trick is to get rid of large and thick roots while retaining the thinner ones that won't show above the soil and will help to retain the plant's health.
- To prepare the right kind of drainage for the bonsai, cover the bottom drainage hole of the pot with a large piece of gravel and then add a thin layer of crushed coal (this helps in the efficient removal of extra moisture from the soil). Top that with a well-draining soil. The composition of soil may vary depending on the plant species used for the bonsai. If you are buying the plant, use the potting mix it came with.
- Add the plant carefully, burying each root gently with a wooden stick (alternatively, use the end of a paintbrush). Use extra soil to hide all the roots and sit the plant firmly upright in the pot.
- As we would do for any kind of repotting, give a few days for the plant to settle in the new pot by placing it in semi-shade conditions for 7–10 days.
- Shift the plant into the desired environmental conditions that it can grow in (this depends on the plant species).
- Once the plant has settled in the new pot and new home, you can now train your plant into a

desired shape and size by trimming the leaves, pruning, wiring and clamping (training to grow in a certain shape), deadwooding (stripping the bark to simulate natural scarring on the tree trunk) and defoliation (removing all the leaves at once). You can use a mix of these techniques or try them individually.

Growing a bonsai into an expected form may take months and years, but the effort is worth the joy.

d. Examples
Look for the hardy and tough wooden stem species, such as Japanese maple, juniper, jade, cedar and weeping fig.

10. HOW TO PROTECT PLANTS FROM EXTREME HEAT
If your plants are burning or shrivelling in the heat, move them to a spot that doesn't compromise on any of the necessary resources (water, light, nutrition and humidity) required by the plant to sustain good growth. Generally, making adjustments to the current space can prove to be more efficient in protecting the plant. Here are some practical suggestions:

a. Add mulch. Cardboard pieces, dried grass, straw, newspaper, sawdust, husk from crops, black plastic sheeting—there is an abundance of options available to cover the soil and reduce water loss.

b. Water in the morning instead of evenings. This will ensure that the roots are well hydrated to sustain

daytime heat waves as the temperatures are relatively lower in the evening or night time.

c. Install shade cloth. Agriculture-grade fabrics can reduce the impact of the sun's heat on the plant by up to 50%. They reduce the rate of water loss and also protect the foliage and flowers from the burning sun.

11. HOW TO PROTECT PLANTS FROM EXTREME COLD

Regions away from the equator may experience single-digit temperatures and even negative temperatures. Unless you are growing a native plant, most others cannot sustain themselves in such conditions. They will not only become dormant but might dry up and die as well. Here are some practices that can come to your plants' rescue:

a. Use mulch. In addition to protecting the plant from the heat, it also helps to retain heat in the ground for longer, especially when the nighttime and daytime temperature fluctuations are major.

b. Cover the plants with a transparent bucket, container or tarp (blue plastic sheet). Ensure that the cover is not in contact with the plant branches as otherwise it can destroy the plant with the gusts of wind.

c. Construct a greenhouse, a permanent enclosure with a covering that does not restrict sunlight but traps heat that can help protect plants from sub-zero temperatures, snow and chilly winds. An artificial heat source can also be included in a greenhouse. If you stay at high altitudes or the temperatures in your region fall below 10°C for a substantial part of the year, investing in a greenhouse can help you get longer growing periods. This will also give you an opportunity to grow a larger variety of plants.

12. HOW TO PROTECT PLANTS FROM TOO MUCH RAIN

Tropical parts of the world see some of the wettest season/s every year. In fact, in some places it may rain over 100 inches a year! To combat the heavy winds and downpour, one can try the following:

a. Use good draining soil which will ensure that there is an escape for standing water that can suffocate the roots and kill your plants.

b. Prune and cover medium to large trees and shrubs. Monsoon undoubtedly leads to the sprouting of much greenery everywhere, but heavy winds—especially in areas near the seas—can take a toll on the plants. After deep pruning of the foliage and side branches, shade net fabric can be wrapped around the plant with a string. This will save the plant from any major physical damage.

c. Add anchors to weak plants to ensure that the plant does not break due to the resistance of the anchor. Use 2–3-feet long bamboo sticks, tied with the main stem of the plant, buried at least 12 inches into the ground. The angle of the stick should be pointing away from the plant (do this angle adjustment before tying the string).

d. Add mulch. Yes, it is the answer to all problems. A heavy downpour may expose the roots and damage

them, but mulch will help reduce the soil displacement and protect the roots.

13. HOW TO WATER PLANTS ON A VACATION

Asking someone to babysit your plants may not be a very practical solution every time you leave them behind. An automatic irrigation system can be super helpful in this regard. Here are some ideas that you can try:

a. Tank and Tube Setup

Requirements: 5–10-litre cans/bottles, a tall stool or a chair, plastic tube whose length and height equal those of the stool, irrigation dripper with adjustable knob and heavy-duty silicone glue

Method

- Make a hole at the base of the water container/can big enough to squeeze the pipe 0.5 inches inside the can. Seal it with the silicone glue.
- On the other end of the pipe, set up the irrigation dripper and fix it in the pot.
  Likewise, you can follow this procedure for other plants as well. Watering frequency can be controlled by the knob on the irrigation dripper. You will have to adjust it in such a way that water comes out drop by drop, neither stagnating in the soil nor drying up. This may not be the most effective way for irrigation, but it is effective for a low budget. Per setup, your expenditure may be not more than 100 rupees.

b. Automated Drip Irrigation

A more efficient, effective and trustworthy version of the tank and tube setup is automated drip irrigation. I use it for my garden because watering over a hundred plants daily not only demands considerable effort but also makes it easier to accidentally leave the plants unattended.

Requirements: Tap/water source, automation regulator, drip irrigation kit (irrigation dripper/emitter, connectors, rubbing, drip emitters, holding sticks).

Method
- Automation regulator is to be connected to the water tap. On its monitor, you can adjust the timing and frequency of watering.
- From the output of the connector, we need to fix the main pipe that will further divide into smaller pipes.
- The smaller pipes are fixed with the emitter that directs water to the base of the plant.

Such setups require minimum human interference unless the water in your area is salt-heavy, which may demand cleaning of the pipes once in a while. My only issue with this method is the cost as one may have to pay a few thousand rupees for the entire kit. However, if you have a lot of plants, you can consider making this investment for your garden at some point.

Notes

PART II

I Was Lying.
It's Also About What You Need.

Chapter 3

ORNAMENTAL PLANTS

Plants that are grown for their attractive leaf colour, leaf shape, bright and deep-coloured flowers are referred to as decorative or ornamental plants. Their life cycle and care may be the same as any other plant, but the focus of their care is to improve the growth of the flower or the leaf. That's their purpose; or, rather, that's their purpose *for you*. Therefore, the growing tips for ornamental plants in Sections 3.1 and 3.2 will emphasize the development of leaves/foliage and flowers respectively.

3.1 FOLIAGE PLANTS

'Indoor Plants' are a popular set of plants purchased in India today. The seller at my local garden centre often tells me how new plant parents come looking for great 'indoor plants' and how he has dedicated real estate to that category. It is, however, a misnomer.

Why, you ask? If you think about it, all plants were doing well 'outdoors' before we humans brought them into our homes and branded them as such. Indoor plant is any plant that can grow well inside our homes—in our living room, bedroom or any similar space.

Imagine a rubber plant, a very common tropical plant. What does it need to grow? Loads of sun (>4 hours of direct sunlight), water whenever the soil dries and regular fertilizer (before you start wondering about the specifics, which I will get into later in the chapter, let me make my point first). While water and fertilizer can be provided in any space, sun is the primary limiting factor that cannot be moved around. Your south-west facing house may get over four hours of direct sunlight daily while my north facing won't get any. In that case, a rubber plant can be an indoor plant for you but will have to be an outdoor plant for me.

I do, in fact, have a better (or more appropriate) name. You can call them foliage plants! These are plants that are grown for their leaves.

Beyond their attractive leaf shape and colour, the fact that makes foliage plants more interesting is that a bunch of these plants have been found to be efficient air purifiers—more than you may think. Hardware and soft furnishings and paints and grease together with smoke coming from factories and vehicles contribute to volatile organic compounds (VOCs). These VOCs include a range of chemicals such as benzene, formaldehyde, xylene and toluene. They are known to be present in the air circulating in indoor spaces such as our bedrooms, living rooms and offices. These chemicals if present in high quantities can cause serious harm to humans. But the good news is that most foliage plants can efficiently remove different VOCs. Yes, plants such as monstera, areca palm, pothos and zz plants can remove pollutants from indoor air.

Insight into plants' abilities to double up as air purifiers comes from an experiment conducted by Dr Bill Wolverton, a NASA scientist who was looking for plants that could help sustain human life in closed spaces with poor air quality (yes, it sounds like research on space-habitation to me too). In a series of experiments using gas chambers, Dr Wolverton found that foliage plants that were commonly growing around his house could eliminate a range of VOCs and improve the air quality. This became a pathbreaking study* and elevated the status of house plants to much more than being just decorative pieces. Some common plants that were used in such experiments were golden pothos, rubber plant, English ivy, monsteras, peace lily, spider plant and snake plant.

If you are wondering what these plants do to remove the pollutants, the answer lies in the term 'rhizosphere'. It is the small area around the plant roots that is immediately

---

* B.C. Wolverton, A. Johnson and K. Bounds, 'Interior landscape plants for indoor air pollution abatement,' NASA/ALCA Final Report, *Plants for Clean Air Council*, Mitchellville, Maryland, 1989.
 B.C. Wolverton and J.D. Wolverton, 'Plants and soil microorganisms—removal of formaldehyde, xylene and ammonia from the indoor environment,' *Journal of the Mississippi Academy of Sciences*, 38 (2): 11–15, 1993.

affected by any root secretions and also consists of millions of microbes living in soil. The air purification studies suggest that this rhizosphere, essentially plants roots and microbes living there, help in the removal of 50–65% of the VOCs. Along with this, plant leaves can also actively absorb, metabolize (fancy word for breakdown) and/or move the VOC to plant roots. The effectiveness of these plants' superhero abilities has been tested for energy-saving and in closed buildings where air circulation is limited and therefore indoor pollution could be higher. For more on this issue, you can read the special report* summarizing various studies carried out in this field.

Honestly, I would not want you to worry too much about which plants are air-purifiers and which ones are not because, if nothing else, any plant will remove CO_2 at the very least. Further, the greenery helps calm our nerves.

General Care

Now, before you leave your house to buy or steal a foliage plant, I have a little checklist for you. I would like you to assess the space where you want to keep a plant first. Since the availability of natural light matters significantly for a plant's healthy growth (discussed in Chapter 1), pay attention to the following factors in your space.

---

* B.C. Wolverton and Mark Nelson, 'Using plants and soil microbes to purify indoor air: lessons from NASA and Biosphere 2 experiments,' *Field Actions Science Reports* Special Issue 21 (2020): 54–59.

☼ Sun

Spend 1–2 days noticing when and how much sun a particular space gets or doesn't get at different times (morning, afternoon and evening) of the day. It doesn't matter if it's the outdoors, indoors, kitchen, bathroom or some other space. You can use the table given below to decide the light availability. This classification will come in handy for growing any kind of plant, from foliage to flowering plants.

How it looks	Common phrases used for reference	Suitable for foliage plants
Open balcony, garden or a room with French windows/big windows. Sun rays fall directly for a large part of the day	Direct sun	✓
East- or west-facing space where rising or dusk sun rays fall directly	Bright light	✓
Sun does not fall directly in the space, but you can comfortably read a book in this space without artificial light	Indirect light/ medium light/ diffused light	✓
Sun does not fall directly in this space. You need artificial light for most of the day	Low light	✓
During the day, there is no natural light. You cannot read a book without artificial light.	Dark	✓ (but fewer options)

TIP: Download any kind of lux metre (device to measure light) app on your smartphone to assess what is the amount of natural light at a given spot. Keep all artificial lights switched off in order to do this. You will be surprised to see how light varies significantly in different spots within the same room. Here are the lux values* I recorded in different spots of my living-cum-dining room, which is south-west facing and on the twelfth floor. Near the window: direct sun/bright light (>1000 lux); around husband's piano area: medium light (100–500 lux); around the dining table: low light (30–80 lux); hall leading to the washroom: dark (<20 lux).

When you apply the abovementioned classification in your space, the lines can be blurry because every house/office is designed differently. The illustration of our living room will help you better understand how I use the light classification to get plants for my living room.

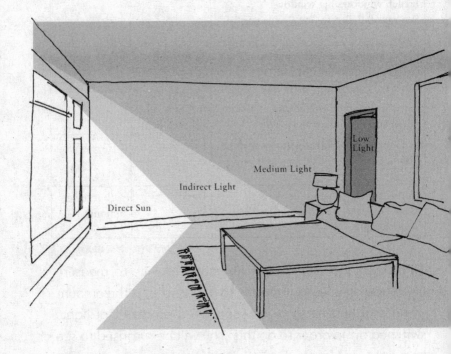

Low Light

Medium Light

Indirect Light

Direct Sun

_____

* These values are just for your reference.

If you are wondering why the introduction to foliage plants is so heavily emphasizing the role of the sun, I would need you to remember that for healthy and happy plants, the most important step is to know how bright or dark your space is. Growing a wrong plant in the wrong kind of light will kill it. End of story. The reason I am obsessing about the sun here is because that's the only factor we cannot move around easily for our plants. Grow lights are of course a great option, but they are also an expensive option and a less convenient setup to grow plants. Since foliage plants are now popularly grown indoors, it is important to understand the light situation you have in your house.

Issues You May Face

Now that I have harped enough on the criticality of light for foliage plants, here are some common symptoms that reflect that the lighting is wrong for your plant.

Symptom: Leaf burn with brown dry spots and/or dry edges

Cause: Overexposure to sun can result in dried edges and leaf burn marks.

Cure: In such a scenario, you should move the plant to a lesser (just a notch lesser) sunny space. If the new leaves that sprout look healthy and green, then the lighting is perfect, but if they continue looking burnt, then you will have to look for more shade.

Symptom: Loss of colour from the leaves

Cause: Insufficient light makes the plant lose colour. Sometimes the plant can turn yellow or the leaves may start looking dull.

Cure: Move the plant to better light conditions.

Some Other Issues That You May Face With Foliage Plants

Symptom: Yellowing of leaves

Cause: Overwatering and underwatering of a plant generally causes yellowing pigmentation of the leaves. Actually, yellowing is a sign that your plant is in stress. A good practice is to start eliminating the reasons that could cause stress to the plant. A logical approach could be inspection, first for watering, then for lighting conditions, then for insects and lastly for fertilizer. When the plant is underwatered, the leaves look paper-dry and yellow. When it is overwatered, leaves will look soggy and yellow. Overwatering may not be easier to point out but underwatered plants first start drooping, and when they are constantly water stressed, they develop dry leaves.

Cure: Water as per the plant's requirements. Most succulents prefer dry soil; their watering requirements are 'low'. Large-leaf tropical plants require 'medium watering', i.e., when the top inch of soil is dry upon touching.

Symptom: Small insects on the leaves and stem

Cause: Mealybugs and spider mites.

Cure: Diluted neem oil spray in the evening on the infected parts. (It's a good practice to read the label before application because I have now started noticing a range of neem oil concentrates available in the market.)

Symptom: Yellow and/or stunted growth

Cause: Low nutrition in the soil.

Cure: Add a good amount of vermicompost or manure every two to three months for boosting plant growth. You can add two handfuls for a medium-sized pot (8–10-inch pot) and scale the portion accordingly for bigger or smaller pots.

🌿 Soil for Foliage Plants

Most plants will do fine in well-draining soil that has equal amounts of cocopeat/perlite, compost and garden soil. In case you can't arrange for this mix, make sure that any soil you use is neither acidic nor alkaline, but has a good dose of organic matter in it and does not hold water for long. Otherwise, the plant will display stunted growth. Furthermore, you can add fertilizer regularly, once every 2–3 months, as most of these plants are 'medium feeders' and enjoy good nutrition.

Plants You Can Grow

In the section below, I have shared a detailed list of foliage plants for three light conditions: bright light, medium light and low light. Plants in each list are arranged according to their ease of care.

A plant that is most tolerant to watering, light and humidity mess-ups is generally referred to as 'an easy plant to grow', whereas the more sensitive it is, the more it is said to be 'difficult to care' for. Plant options given below have been offered keeping beginners and plant serial-killers in mind. They are arranged in order of difficulty in the list, with the first plant being the easiest of all to care for. In fact, you can consider the top five plants in each category to be the easiest ones to care for. It is worth mentioning that this ease or difficulty is based on my personal experiences of growing them in cities that I have lived in: Bangalore, Delhi, Faridabad and Mumbai.

Ten to Know

Bright Light

1. Rubber Plant

Suitable Conditions for Good Growth

☀ *Sun:* Direct sun
🗐 *Water:* Medium watering
🗓 *Soil:* Regular soil mix
🌡 *Temperature:* Medium-high
🍴 *Fertilizer:* Medium feeder

Common Varieties

Burgundy rubber plant (*Ficus elastica* 'Burgundy'), common rubber plant (*Ficus elastica* 'Robusta') and variegated rubber plant (*Ficus elastica* 'Tricolor')

Grow For: Air-purifying qualities

Aesthetics: Burgundy rubber plant develops a deep maroon colour, and the variegated rubber plant variety shows a beautiful amalgamation of pink, green and cream colours. When provided with the right conditions, they can also grow up to 8 ft in a pot and 50 ft or more in deep soil.

Common Issues: Leaf burn and loss of colour

Propagation: Cutting with rooting hormone method

Super Tip: Support the length of the stem using a stick and trim the plant regularly to help it grow erect and bushy. Snipping the tip initiates side growth, making the plant grow more laterally (side stems) instead of one lanky tall stem.

2. Palms

Suitable Conditions for Good Growth

- ☼ *Sun:* Direct sun-Bright light
- ⬦ *Water:* Medium watering
- ⬥ *Soil:* Regular soil mix
- 🌡 *Temperature:* Medium-high
- 🍴 *Fertilizer:* Medium feeder

Common Varieties

Areca palm (*Dypsis lutescens*), rhapis palm (*Rhapis excelsa*), fan palm (*Livistona chinensis*), ponytail palm (*Beaucarnea recurvata*)

Grow For: Air-purifying qualities and aesthetics

Common Issues: Leaf burn and white powdery insects

Propagation: Separate a plant pup/plant offset along with some intact roots from a bunch. Most palms can also be grown from seeds, but since the germination is slow and the success rate is low, the divide-and-grow method works best.

Super Tip: Areca and rhapis are the easier ones to grow. They like the fine balance between soil moisture and bright light. In the absence of either, they may turn yellow. However, I still consider them 'easy to care for' because once you correct the watering and lighting, the plant adjusts quickly and sends out new healthy growth.

3. Dracaena

Suitable Conditions for Good Growth

☀ *Sun:* Direct sun/bright light
🪣 *Water:* Medium watering
🪴 *Soil:* Regular soil mix
🌡 *Temperature:* Medium
🍴 *Fertilizer:* Medium feeder

Common Varieties

Dragon tree (*Dracaena marginata),*
mass cane (*Dracaena massangeana*), dracaena lemon lime (*Dracaena deremensis* 'Lemon Lime')

Grow For

- **Aesthetics:** With one or two central stems and a big bunch of leaves on the top, this plant is an interesting piece of decor. Its shape can also be easily manipulated with regular pruning. The dragon tree especially ages beautifully, with the trunk moulding and folding with time.

Common Issues

- **Droopy lower leaves:** A common problem when it receives a lesser dose of light than it needs.
- **Slow growth:** It is naturally a slow-growing plant, but it starts looking lush and green within the first year when it is about a foot tall.

Propagation: Stem cutting with rooting hormone

Super Tip: Dracaena also flowers if kept in good light and with perfect watering, which is 'just barely moist soil'.

4. Curtain Creeper

Suitable Conditions for Good Growth

- ☼ *Sun:* Bright light
- 💧 *Water:* Medium watering
- 🪴 *Soil:* Regular soil mix
- 🌡 *Temperature:* Medium
- 🍴 *Fertilizer:* Medium feeder

Common Variety: Curtain creeper
(*Tarlmounia elliptica*)

Grow For
- **Aesthetics:** Live, green, vertical fencing that grows quickly

Common Issues
- **Irregular and untamed growth:** This plant might start growing in random directions wherever it finds support. Sometimes a patch of the stems might start drying suddenly. In both cases, regular pruning and structural support (in a mesh design, preferably) will help.

Propagation: Stem cutting in soil. Usage of rooting hormone improves chances of successful propagation.

Super Tip: Regular washing with a spray of water gives the curtain creeper a fresh and lush look. I recommend

planting the saplings directly in soil around the monsoon season (preferably during the retreat of the monsoon), especially if you stay in a hot place. This will allow the plant to grow and establish itself before the intense summer season returns.

#FUNFACT: *Tarlmounia elliptica or curtain creeper, popularly known as parda bel, is native to India. Terms such as 'indigenous species' or 'native' are commonly used by scientists to imply that this particular species was not introduced from anywhere outside but perhaps first originated in this region, thus describing its place of origin. Please note: You have perhaps noticed the usage of terms like 'seems', 'perhaps' and 'appears' for describing such scientific concepts in this book. This is because they are mostly deductions that are made from genetic studies done in labs. However, as the scientific tools become more sophisticated and the understanding of genomes (genetic makeup) improves steadily, we may learn later that our understanding might have been partially or completely wrong.*

For example, we have recently learned that a plant called 'mother-in-law's tongue' which was thought to be a Sansevieria species is actually a kind of a Dracaena species. To cite another example, termites, which were thought to be a different order of insects, are now found to be actually a kind of cockroach (this is my personal favourite because my doctoral research largely involved termites. During the course of my research, this reclassification of termites happened—a big thing in the scientific community. This finding also totally changed my perspective on termites). Intriguing, right? Anyway, let's go back to plants.

5. Kalanchoe

Suitable Conditions for Good Growth

☀ *Sun:* Bright light
💧 *Water:* Low watering
🌱 *Soil:* Succulent soil mix
🌡 *Temperature:* Medium
🍴 *Fertilizer:* Rare feeder

Common Varieties

Supermarket kalanchoe
(*Kalanchoe blossfeldiana*), wavy-leaf
red-tip kalanchoe (*Kalanchoe luciae*),
mother of thousands (*Kalanchoe laetivirens*)

Grow For

- Aesthetics: It has waxy, broad leaves and some varieties also show gorgeous red shades. A small kalanchoe can be used to style a coffee table or a bookshelf.

Common Issues

- Soggy and yellow leaves: It is a succulent plant which means that it is vulnerable to overwatering. Continued overwatering can make leaves lose colour, become soggy and eventually die.

Propagation: The stem-cutting method works best for *Kalanchoe blossfeldiana*. The other two varieties (*Kalanchoe luciae* and *Kalanchoe laetivirens*) can be easily grown using snipped offsets or pups planted in soil (divide and grow method). Stem cutting method will also work for the latter two varieties, but the success rate might be lesser as compared to the divide and grow method.

Super Tip: Kalanchoe grows and sends out beautiful flowers if placed in a space with bright, direct sunlight. If the plant is light deprived, flowering will be rare and will only grow vegetatively.

> #FUNFACT: 'Succulent' is a term used for any plant that has adapted over several generations to grow in dry, desert-like conditions. The interesting part is that you can actually observe some adaptations with naked eyes. You would need an aloe vera plant and a knife.*
>
> Split open one of the aloe leaves from the centre. You would find a gel-like substance. It is the unique ability of this plant to store water in its leaves to sustain long dry spells. In fact, I find the aloe plant to be a great example to see succulent adaptations—thick leaves with a waxy surface to conserve water together with sharp edges to protect the soft part of the plant from herbivores like sheep and cows.

In succulents, apart from these visible features, plants like aloe vera also have a very interesting photosynthesis system, one which is different from most other plants. Succulents, unlike other plants, take in carbon dioxide only at night. They store that carbon dioxide at night and use it in the daytime when the sun comes out to process their food. The oxygen which is then produced is stored in the plant during the day and is released during the night. This pattern helps in reducing the loss of water from the plant. Remember: their natural habitat is a desert. If the plant would have opened its pores for gas

---

* Caution recommended. Not recommended for children without adult supervision.

exchange during the day when the sun is most intense, that would have increased the loss of moisture too. And moisture is a rare resource in an arid area that must be protected at all costs. This mechanism is called the C4* pathway of photosynthesis where the exchange of carbon dioxide and oxygen happens only at night when the sun is down.

Also note that the abovementioned process of photosynthesis does not imply that succulents are a great source of oxygen at night. In that respect, this process is quite inefficient. Scientific experiments have shown that the oxygen that ultimately comes out during the night is very low or negligible to call these plants sources of oxygen at night. My point is please don't fall for commercial gimmicks that sell succulents as a source of oxygen at night in your bedroom.

6. Jade

Suitable Conditions for Good Growth

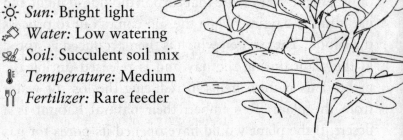

☼ *Sun:* Bright light
💧 *Water:* Low watering
🌱 *Soil:* Succulent soil mix
🌡 *Temperature:* Medium
🍴 *Fertilizer:* Rare feeder

---

* C4 = Four carbon chemical structure of the carbohydrate formed in this process.

Common Varieties: Button plant/jade plant (*Crassula arborescens* and *Crassula ovata*) and dwarf jade (*Portulacaria afra*)

Grow For: Aesthetics and ease of growing

Common Issues
- Dropping leaves: Constant brushing against the plant and overwatering are the main culprits resulting in the shedding of leaves

Propagation: Stem cuttings propagated in soil

Super Tip: Since this is a succulent, exposure to a good amount of sun (>3hours) and slight water stress can help the leaves look glossy. Under good sunlight, the sunset jade also develops an orange shade on the edges. Some species, such as the *Portulacaria* species, can be trained to grow like a bonsai plant and take interesting shapes.

#FUNFACT: *Most animals and plants have two names: a common name and a scientific name (always written in italics, if done right). Common names have better recall whereas scientific names are complicated and difficult to remember. However, common names can also be confusing. For example, 'jade' or 'button plant' are common names primarily used for the Crassula species. However, some people also use them to refer to Portulacaria species because of the resemblance in their small round leaves. For gardening beginners, it's a challenge to distinguish between them. Thankfully, both these species have similar requirements in terms of sun, water and soil, so it doesn't matter after all. However, for plants like lucky bamboo—which is actually not a bamboo—the common name can be misleading for the uninitiated. Its requirements are nothing like the real bamboo. We will talk about the lucky bamboo in the following pages.*

7. Alocasia

Suitable Conditions for Good Growth

☀ *Sun:* Bright light
🪣 *Water:* Wet feet
🌱 *Soil:* Regular soil mix
🌡 *Temperature:* Medium
🍴 *Fertilizer:* Regular heavy feeder

Common Varieties: Alocasia or elephant ear or taro plant (*Alocasia Amazonica, Alocasia wentii* and *Alocasia cuprea* 'Red Secret')

Grow For

- Aesthetics: Elephant ear-like leaves make alocasia a great decor piece, and the wide variety of this species ranges in height—from a 6 foot giant taro to a few inches tall *Alocasia cuprea* 'Red Secret'.

Common Issues: Browning of leaves and spider mites

Propagation: Stem cuttings can be propagated in soil for *K. blossfeldiana*. The divide and grow method works for all kinds of Alocasias.

Super Tip: This plant's leaves mature quickly. It also grows new leaves at a fast rate. Therefore, regular removal of matured leaves helps it look great in living spaces.

8. Fiddle-Leaf Fig

Suitable Conditions for Good Growth

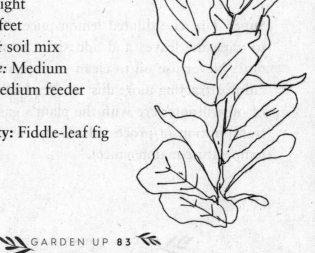

☼ *Sun:* Bright light
◇ *Water:* Wet feet
🪴 *Soil:* Regular soil mix
🌡 *Temperature:* Medium
🍴 *Fertilizer:* Medium feeder

Common Variety: Fiddle-leaf fig (*Ficus lyrata*)

Grow For

- Aesthetics: Like most figs, it develops broad and shiny leaves. Additionally, it can grow up to 15 feet indoors in a medium-sized pot. It is very popular among home decorators; in fact, some famous decor stores also sell its polyester version.
- Air-purifying qualities: It can help reduce mould from indoor spaces.

Common Issues

- Brown edges: These develop either due to fungus infestation or low indoor humidity. In fact, this problem of brown edges is my main reason for not keeping fiddle-leaf fig at the top of this list of plants. For fiddle-leaf fig, one needs to constantly watch out for drying leaves and address that immediately, especially as the seasons change.

Propagation: Stem cutting propagation in water as well as cutting with rooting hormone planted in soil methods work for propagation.

Super Tip: Use diluted lemon juice on a cotton cloth to wipe the leaves and add shine to the plant. Please note: Never use oil to clean your plants. First, oil will aid in attracting more dust to the plant. Second, a layer of oil will interfere with the plant's gas exchanges and transpiration (a process that helps in evaporation and temperature maintenance).

9. Ficus Benjamina

Suitable Conditions for Good Growth

☼ *Sun:* Bright light
🪣 *Water:* Wet feet
🪴 *Soil:* Regular soil mix
🌡 *Temperature:* Medium
🍴 *Fertilizer:* Heavy feeder

Common Varieties: Weeping fig/ficus plant or ficus tree (*Ficus benjamina*)

Grow For: Aesthetics and ease of growing

Common Issues: Stunted growth

Propagation: Stem-cutting method

Super Tip: It's a great plant to grow as a hedge or for fencing. You can use it to add some privacy in a highrise balcony as well as for a piece of land.

10. Cacti

Suitable Conditions for Good Growth

☀ *Sun:* Bright
✎ *Water:* Low
🌱 *Soil:* Regular potting mix
🌡 *Temperature:* High
🍴 *Fertilizer:* Low

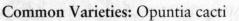

Common Varieties: Opuntia cacti
(*Opuntia ficus-indica* and *Opuntia microdasys*), cereus cacti (*Selenicereus grandiflorus*) and echinocactus cacti (*Echinocactus grusonii*)

> #FUNFACT: *All cacti (plural)/cactus (singular) are succulents, but all succulents are not cacti! The term 'cactus' is derived from an ancient Greek word κάκτος (kaktos), which means a plant with spines. The presence of spines is an adaptation that helps to survive dry regions. Spines help plants in three ways primarily: (1) defend the plant from herbivores, (2) collect condensed vapours of water during the cool nighttime and (3) radiate heat during the hot daytime.*

Grow For

- Low maintenance: You can add water once in a fortnight and forget about them. Additionally, they are great for craft DIY projects such as terrariums.

Common Issues

- **Slow death:** They might die in a few days if subjected to continuous overwatering. Also remember that they are naturally slow growers. Watering them constantly or fertilizing them will not help them grow bigger quickly.

Propagation: Remove the pups that have a few roots and repot them in a new pot.

Super Tip: If you stay in a dry region, you can make a succulent garden with coloured gravel, big stones, porcelain props and different kinds of cacti.

Ten to Know

Medium light

1. Croton

Suitable Conditions for Good Growth

☼ *Sun:* Medium-bright light
🖑 *Water:* Medium watering
🌿 *Soil:* Regular soil mix
🌡 *Temperature:* Medium-high
🍴 *Fertilizer:* Medium feeder

Common Variety: Croton
(*Codiaeum variegatum*)

Grow For

- Aesthetics: Great for adding colour, especially in places where you can't easily grow flowers.

Common Issues: Mealybugs

Propagation: Cutting with rooting hormone method

Super Tip: Crotons can sustain well in medium light, but moving them to a brighter area will help their pigmentation become deeper, thereby making the plant look more colourful.

2. Aglaonema

Suitable Conditions for Good Growth

☀ *Sun:* Medium-low light
🔧 *Water:* Medium watering
🌱 *Soil:* Regular soil mix
🌡 *Temperature:* Low-medium
🍴 *Fertilizer:* Medium feeder

Common Varieties: Green Philippine evergreen (*Aglaonema commutatum*), aglaonema pink dalmatian (*Aglaonema commutatum* 'Pink Dalmatian')

Grow For: Aesthetics

Common Issues: Brown and dry edges

Propagation: Divide and grow method

Super Tip: The green aglaonema is the easiest to grow and can sustain well even in low light conditions. Just like in crotons, bright light helps with deep leaf pigmentation, but protect the plant from intense noon sunlight.

3. Philodendrons

Suitable Conditions for Good Growth

☀ *Sun:* Medium-low light
💦 *Water:* Medium watering
🪴 *Soil:* Regular soil mix
🌡 *Temperature:* Low-high
🍴 *Fertilizer:* Medium feeder

Common Varieties: Velvet-leaf philodendron (*Philodendron micans*), winterbourn (*Philodendron xanadu),* red-leaf philodendron (*Philodendron erubescens*), heartleaf philodendron (*Philodendron oxycardium*)

Grow For
- Hangings: They look great in hanging baskets, especially in coir-lined baskets which help them grow better and retain moisture longer.

Common Issues: Yellowing of the leaves

Propagation: Stem cutting method

Super Tip: Use a moss stick for better growth as it can retain moisture for longer. Philodendrons, like pothos, send out aerial roots that can absorb moisture from the moss stick, thereby helping the plant grow faster and with bigger leaves.

4. Monsteras

Suitable Conditions for Good Growth

☀ *Sun:* Medium-bright light
💧 *Water:* Wet feet
🪴 *Soil:* Regular soil mix
🌡 *Temperature:* Medium-high
🍴 *Fertilizer:* Regular heavy feeder

Common Varieties: Split-leaf monstera (*Monstera deliciosa*), swiss cheese monstera/monstera with holes (*Monstera adansonii*)

Grow For
- Aesthetics: All monstera species have very interesting leaf shapes. In recent years, it has become a decor magazine favourite. In all boho-themed interiors, you might spot a monstera somewhere.

Common Issues: Brown tips and yellowing of leaves.

Propagation: Stem cutting method. Cut under the node like you would do for any cutting, but also include at least one aerial root in the cutting. This root will help develop more roots, speeding up the propagation.

Super Tip: Use a wire mesh on a wall to turn it into a green wall. Monstera's aerial roots will help it climb the support and form a lush green wall.

5. Wandering Jew

Suitable Conditions for Good Growth

☼ *Sun:* Medium-bright light
💧 *Water:* Medium
🪴 *Soil:* Regular soil mix
🌡 *Temperature:* Medium
🍴 *Fertilizer:* Regular heavy feeder

Common Varieties: Wandering jew (*Tradescantia zebrina*, formerly recognized as *Zebrina pendula*)

Grow For
- Aesthetics: Its purple-coloured and green-coloured leaves look beautiful as a hanging plant.

Common Issues

- Loss of purple colour: If the plant is not getting enough light, it will start losing the purple pigment and turn green. Keep the plant in a space with bright-medium light, but avoid any direct sunlight as otherwise it will turn brown.

Propagation: Stem cutting method

Super Tip: Use a room humidifier to make this plant grow rapidly and flourish indoors. It does not like moist soil but loves high humidity in the surroundings.

6. Anthurium

Suitable Conditions for Good Growth

☀ *Sun:* Medium-low light
💧 *Water:* Medium
🪴 *Soil:* Regular soil mix
🌡 *Temperature:* Medium
🍴 *Fertilizer:* Regular heavy feeder

Common Variety: Anthurium plant (*Anthurium andraeanum*). This plant looks very similar to peace lily, but it is more hardy and tolerant than peace lily.

Grow For

- Aesthetics: Red and white flowers (there are very few flowering plants that can be grown in medium light conditions).

Common Issues

- No or few flowers: Light-deprived conditions can reduce flowering in the plant. Keeping the plant in a brighter space where there is enough light to read a book but no direct sunlight will help stimulate flower growth.
- Low flower pigment: Actually, this is not a problem per se. Some subspecies show very intense red colour whereas some develop a pale red/pink colour.

Propagation: Can be grown from seeds as well as stem cutting in soil or water. However, the success rate might be lower with both the methods mentioned above, in which case the divide and grow method can be used.

Super Tip: Despite all measures, if the anthurium is not flowering, add a handful of steamed fish bone meal to a medium-sized pot (8–10-inch deep pot), prune the tips of the plant and keep outdoors in an east- or west-facing balcony. The bright (but not intense) morning or evening sun can help stimulate flower growth, and then you can bring it back to medium light conditions.

7. Prayer Plant

Suitable Conditions for Good Growth

☀ *Sun:* Medium-low light
✎ *Water:* Medium
✽ *Soil:* Regular soil mix
🌡 *Temperature:* Medium
🍴 *Fertilizer:* Regular heavy feeder

Common Varieties: *Calathea* and *Maranta* species.
Peacock plant (*Calathea makoyana*), rattlesnake plant (*Calathea lancifolia*) and prayer plant (*Maranta leuconeura*).

Grow For
- Aesthetics: Their leaves have beautiful patterns and colours, and they show an interesting phenomenon called 'Nyctinasty', where the leaves fold during night time and open during the day.

Common Issues: Burnt leaf edges

Propagation: Divide and grow method

Super Tip: These plants prefer places which are humid but close to dry soil. Therefore, keeping all your prayer plants together around a humidifier will help them grow better and look healthier.

8. Ivy

Suitable Conditions for Good Growth

☀ *Sun:* Medium-low light
💧 *Water:* Medium
🌱 *Soil:* Regular soil mix
🌡 *Temperature:* Medium
🍴 *Fertilizer:* Regular heavy feeder

Common Varieties: English ivy
(*Hedera helix*) and glacier ivy
(*Hedera helix* 'Glacier')

Grow For: Aesthetics and air purifying abilities

Common Issues
- Slow drying of the plant: In my experience, I have found that this plant is very sensitive to temperature and light availability. If either of them is changed and if the plant does not like the new spot, it might dry up overnight. Be cautious of which spot you choose to keep this plant (medium light and medium temperature)

Propagation: Stem cutting with rooting hormone method.
For plants like ivy that have soft stems and are sensitive to water availability, propagation in river sand works better than in regular soil because the former ensures good drainage, thereby reducing the occurrence of root rot.

Super Tip: If you need to cover a wall for any reason, use a pigeon net secured with nails on the wall and allow the ivy plant to climb upon it. Within 5–6 months, you will have a completely green and luscious wall.

9. Ferns

Suitable Conditions for Good Growth

☼ *Sun:* Medium-low light
💧 *Water:* Medium
🪴 *Soil:* Regular soil mix
🌡 *Temperature:* Medium
🍴 *Fertilizer:* Heavy feeder

Common Varieties: Boston fern (*Nephrolepis exaltata*), bird's nest fern *(Asplenium nidus)* and maiden fern (*Adiantum raddianum*)

Grow For: Aesthetics and air-purifying qualities.

Common Issues
- Drying of plants: Ferns are extremely sensitive (most sensitive being maiden fern and most hardy being the bird's nest) to temperature (20–30°C) and humidity (>50%). Any changes in either of them may make the leaves turn brown. Adding an artificial humidifier will help keep ferns healthy and green.

Propagation: Dividing and repotting method

Super Tip: In a highrise building with exposed balcony space and intense sunlight, place the ferns under bigger plants. This will help reduce the intensity of sunlight falling on the plant, thereby keeping the temperature lower than ambient temperature and humidity higher than ambient humidity.

10. Caladiums

Suitable Conditions for Good Growth

☀ *Sun:* Medium-low light
✎ *Water:* Medium-high
🌱 *Soil:* Regular soil mix
🌡 *Temperature:* Medium
🍴 *Fertilizer:* Regular heavy feeder

Grow For
- Aesthetics: The coloured, delicate-looking caladium leaves make them suitable for a perfect decor piece.

Common Varieties: Caladium plant (*Caladium bicolor*). Within this species, there are several subspecies that offer a range of colours, from pink to deep maroon to pale green.

Common Issues
- Drying of the plant: Caladium, like ferns, are sensitive to their microclimate. High temperature (>25°C) and low humidity (<50%) can make the leaves turn

brown or even kill the plant overnight. They do best during the monsoon season.

- Another factor that can silently kill caladiums is bad drainage. Ensure that water does not stand in the pot when you add water.

Propagation: You can purchase bulbs to grow caladium. However, I recommend following the divide and repotting method which has a better success rate.

Super Tip: If the leaves start losing their bright colours, try to move the plant to a brighter and humid space at the earliest as otherwise it will die quickly.

Ten to Know

Low light

Before I discuss the plants in this category, I would like to clarify that every plant needs some light. Light is an important requisite for photosynthesis, the process of making food in plants. Prolonged exposure to absolute darkness for any plant can lead to its death. In the section below, I have listed plants that can survive in spaces in low light conditions. However, please treat them like they are on life-support, since any mess-ups in their water and temperature requirement can lead to quick yellowing or dying. I recommend moving such plants every month to medium light conditions for a week at least so that they can catch up on their growth.

1. Snake Plant

Suitable Conditions for Good Growth

☼ *Sun:* Low-medium light
🖊 *Water:* Low watering
🔱 *Soil:* Succulent-type soil mix
🌡 *Temperature:* Medium
🍴 *Fertilizer:* Rare feeder

Common Varieties: Mother-in-law's tongue or snake plant (*Dracaena trifasciata*). There are several subspecies of this plant such as *Dracaena trifasciata* 'Black Gold', *Dracaena trifasciata* 'Futura Robusta', *Dracaena trifasciata* 'Futura Superba', *Dracaena trifasciata* 'Cylindrica', to name a few.

Grow For
- Low maintenance: There is no other plant that needs such minimal water and can sustain itself in such low light conditions.
- Air-purifying abilities.

Common Issues: Soggy leaves and yellowing of leaves. Avoid overwatering.

Propagation: Cut one leaf into 5–6-inch pieces and pot the lower end of the leaf in soil 3–4 cm deep. Water the soil on the seventh day of potting the leaves, and water only once in a month. This plant may take 1–2 months to show roots.

Super Tip: Since this plant is the most tolerant one among low low-light, it does well in dark hallways and bathrooms too.

2. ZZ Plant

Suitable Conditions for Good Growth

- ☀ *Sun:* Low-medium light
- 💧 *Water:* Low
- 🌱 *Soil:* Succulent-type soil mix
- 🌡 *Temperature:* Medium
- 🍴 *Fertilizer:* Rare feeder

Common Variety: ZZ plant (*Zamioculcas zamiifolia*). This plant has two subspecies: a black one (raven ZZ plant) and green one (green ZZ plant).

Common Issues: Yellowing of leaves. Improving lighting and water will help in recovery.

Propagation: Divide and grow method works best, but you can also try taking a stem cutting and putting it in water to root.

Super Tip: Use the bouquet sponge to propagate plants like the ZZ plant and snake plant. Insert the leaf cuttings gently in the wet sponge. As the bouquet sponge is capable of holding water for long, it will work effectively for plants that take months to develop root callus, thereby giving them just enough moisture but without rot. Wet the sponge once a fortnight.

3. Pothos

Suitable Conditions for Good Growth

☀ *Sun:* Medium-low light
🪣 *Water:* Medium watering
🪴 *Soil:* Regular soil mix
🌡 *Temperature:* Low-high
🍴 *Fertilizer:* Medium feeder

Common Varieties: Golden pothos (*Epipremnum aureum*), marble queen pothos (*Epipremnum aureum* 'Marble Queen'), manjula pothos (*Epipremnum aureum* 'Manjula').
Pothos have an abundance of varieties that are easily available and convenient to grow. To a beginner, they may all look the same, but that is completely okay because the care is the same and all that matters is that you like the plant and can cater to its needs.

Grow For
- Ease of maintenance: Even when you think that you might have killed the plant, it can be brought back to life by mending the watering and light availability.
- Air-purifying qualities: Experiments show that pothos are capable of removing volatile organic compounds (VOCs) such as toluene and benzene.

Common Issues

- Yellow leaves and blackening of leaves. Blackening is caused by fungal attack, common in plants that are constantly overwatered.

Propagation: Stem-cutting method

Super Tip: Regularly cut the tips of the plant. This will help in side growth, thereby making it grow bushy.

4. Lucky Bamboo

Suitable Conditions for Good Growth

☀ *Sun:* Medium-low light
💧 *Water:* Medium watering
🪴 *Soil:* Regular soil mix. They easily grow in plain water too
🌡 *Temperature:* Low-high
🍴 *Fertilizer:* Medium feeder

Common Variety: Lucky bamboo is actually not a bamboo, but a kind of dracaena plant (*Dracaena sanderiana*).

Grow For

- Ease of maintenance: Keep the stems of lucky bamboo in water in a glass jar. Fill the base with gravel, and you have a live decor piece to decorate your bathroom.

Common Issues

- Root rot: Lucky bamboo growing in water is highly prone to fungal attacks/root rot. If you notice some of its stem yellowing and drying, remove the yellowed stems and wash the healthier stem in running water once a week every month. Further, to help the plant recover faster, keep it in a medium light space.

Propagation: Stem cutting taken from the node can be propagated both in water or directly in soil.

Super Tip: By manipulating the light availability, lucky bamboo stems can be grown in a spiral shape.

Here is how to go about it:

- Take a cardboard box the length of your plant and remove one of the sides along the length of the box.
- Place bamboo sticks inside the box.
- Now, keep the box in such a way that its open side faces a light source (not the top).
- Continue caring for your plant as before, until the tip of the plant growing out of the exposed side of the box starts leaning towards the light source.
- As you keep rotating the plant, it will continue to grow towards the light source, and if you continue spinning in the same direction, the sticks will eventually start looking spiral shaped.

5. Fittonia

Suitable Conditions for Good Growth

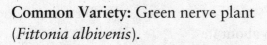

- ☀ *Sun:* Medium-low light
- ✎ *Water:* Wet feet
- 🌿 *Soil:* Regular soil mix. They can be easily grown in plain water too.
- 🌡 *Temperature:* Low-medium
- 🍴 *Fertilizer:* Medium feeder

Common Variety: Green nerve plant (*Fittonia albivenis*).

Grow For

- Aesthetics: The intricate nerve-like pattern can make it a great table-decor piece. However, it is a borderline low light-medium light plant. It will need a close watch if kept in interior parts of the house where natural light is restricted.

Common Issues

- Drooping leaves: The leaves and stems are delicate and sensitive to water availability. As the soil starts to dry up, the leaves will also start drooping.

Propagation: Divide and grow method

Super Tip: As the fittonias prefer moist soil, you can use old coffee mugs without drainage holes to grow them. Water only when the leaves start drooping.

6. Peace Lily

Suitable Conditions for Good Growth

- ☀ *Sun:* Medium-low light
- ✎ *Water:* Wet feet
- ✑ *Soil:* Regular soil mix
- 🌡 *Temperature:* Low-high
- 🍴 *Fertilizer:* Medium feeder

Common Variety: Peace lily (*Spathiphyllum wallisii, Spathiphyllum kochii, Spathiphyllum silvicola*). They are all different species, but they almost look the same, so there is no need to pay much attention to the scientific name because the care remains the same.

Grow For
- Aesthetics: It is a rare indoor plant that flowers easily.
- Air-purifying capabilities: It was among the list of plants that were first tested in the NASA study that looked at foliage plants' ability to purify air. Peace lily turned out to remove three major VOCs—benzene, carbon monoxide and formaldehyde.

Common Issues

- Yellow and brown tips: It's a very sensitive plant. Any mistakes with watering can lead to yellowing or browning.

Propagation: Divide and grow method.

Super Tip: Peace lily does fine in low light, but to initiate frequent flowering, move it next to a window.

7. Aspidistra

Suitable Conditions for Good Growth

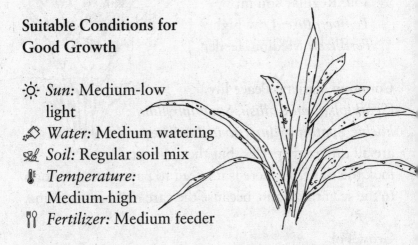

- ☼ *Sun:* Medium-low light
- ✎ *Water:* Medium watering
- ✿ *Soil:* Regular soil mix
- 🌡 *Temperature:* Medium-high
- 🍴 *Fertilizer:* Medium feeder

Common Variety: Aspidistra (*Aspidistra yingjiangensis*). There are a number of species of aspidistra, and some of them in fact look very similar to peace lily. However, I want you to try *Aspidistra yingjiangensis* 'Singapore Sling' specifically because it does best in low light conditions as compared to others.

Grow For: Aesthetics

Common Issues
- Rare to find: Aspidistra has still not become very popular in Indian markets, so you may face a little challenge in sourcing it.

Propagation: Divide and grow method

Super Tip: Its leaves are long and hardy. To make the plant look tall, collect the leaves and tie them around a wooden stick with a thread.

8. Syngonium

Suitable Conditions for Good Growth

☀ *Sun:* Medium-low light
💧 *Water:* Medium watering. They can grow in plain water as well
🪴 *Soil:* Regular soil mix
🌡 *Temperature:* Low-medium
🍴 *Fertilizer:* Medium feeder

Common Variety: Arrowhead vine (*Syngonium podophyllum*).

Grow For

- Aesthetics: Unlike most other vining plants, arrowhead is a vine with a thicker stem that enables it to conveniently climb against a wall or a fence.

Common Issues: Yellow and brown tip of leaves

Propagation: Stem cutting taken from the node propagated both in water or directly in soil

Super Tip: If for any reason you have killed the plant, don't lose hope. As long as the roots of syngonium are alive in soil, it can bounce back to life with regular watering.

9. Rhoeo Plant

Suitable Conditions for
Good Growth

- ☼ *Sun:* Medium-low light
- 🪣 *Water:* Medium watering. They can grow in plain water as well
- 🪱 *Soil:* Regular soil mix
- 🌡 *Temperature:* Low-medium
- 🍽 *Fertilizer:* Medium feeder

Common Variety: Rhoeo or boat lily (*Tradescantia spathacea*)

Grow For

- Aesthetics: Its purple colour makes this plant among the few plants that have coloured leaves/foliage, thereby making it great for table tops and countertops.

Common Issues

- Loss of purple colour: If deprived of light, the leaves will use their purple pigmentation and turn green.

Propagation: Stem cutting method

Super Tip: Recycle an old fruit basket by lining it with a layer of polythene with 3–4 holes at the base for drainage and use cocopeat-based potting mix to grow this plant. Since rhoeo do not demand much water and care, they will grow easily in such baskets.

#FUNFACT: *Wonder why some plants like Rhoeo are not green in colour?*

The colour of anything in this world is dependent on what wavelength of the light spectrum that object reflects back. As we discussed in Chapter 1, plant leaves generally absorb all the regions of the spectrum except green, thereby making the plants 'look' green to our eyes. The pigment that contributes to the reflection of that green light is called chlorophyll.

However, plants like rhoeo or wandering jew that look purple have other pigments such as anthocyanin that reflect some part of the blue region of the light spectrum, thereby making the leaves look purple. These plants will also have chlorophyll in them, but the amount will be relatively lower as compared to an absolutely green plant.

10. Tillandsia Species

Suitable Conditions for Good Growth

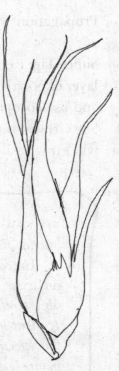

- ☀ *Sun:* Medium-low light
- *Water:* Water spray daily
- *Soil:* Not required
- *Temperature:* Low-medium
- *Fertilizer:* Not required

Common Varieties: Air plant (*Tillandsia ionantha* and *Tillandsia seleriana*) and Spanish moss (*Tillandsia usneoides*)

Grow For

- Aesthetics: Tillandsia species come in large varieties: some are small, some are big and some look like moss too. Since these plants do not need soil to grow, you can literally plant them anywhere.

Common Issues

- Dries quickly: Tillandsias are used to growing on trees in rainforests. Therefore, they love lots of humidity, in the absence of which they start dying.
- Another issue—actually, a fact—about these plants is that they die post flowering. The flower will remain on the plant for long but once it dries, the plant also starts drying in most cases.

Propagation: If you are lucky to get a pup coming out of the base of your tillandsia, you can separate and grow it as a new plant.

Super Tip: Air plants give you freedom to use them for creative projects. You can use stones, bark or anything to glue the air plant on it for indoor decor ideas.

3.2 FLOWERING PLANTS

Flowers evoke emotions. I am not a poet, and I will not try to be one (trying to be a writer is hard enough for me), but I do have things to say about flowers. Their fragrance and their colours have made me spend hours appreciating nature and its wonders. They come in a range of shades, shapes, sizes, fragrances; some bloom during the day, some bloom at night, some bloom in winter, some in summer, others round the year . . . the list can go on. Their wide variety offers endless options to feel a hundred different ways or, much more simply, to decorate your space.

To make your little balcony colourful, bring in a bunch of sunflowers, roses and marigolds. To make your

living room smell wonderful naturally, grow a bunch of mogras on the windowsill. You can grow flowers in pots and on the ground. You can recycle any kind of container and make it special by growing flowers in it. If you have more than a few square metres of land, first of all—congratulations (for people like me staying in Mumbai, that's an alien concept), and second, you can consider developing raised beds to grow flowers. Imagine waking up to the sight of daisies, lilies, orchids and marigolds swaying in your garden and bees and butterflies hovering on them.

For a home with a patch of land, raised beds (*see box*) could be a good way to grow any kind of plants as they help keep weeds at bay and make soil amendments for plants much easier.

What is a raised bed?
As the name suggests, it is a part of a garden raised slightly higher than the actual level of that land. Raised beds allow you to grow both flowers and veggies aesthetically while utilizing large spaces effectively at the same time. Selecting patches of land to form raised beds will give you an opportunity to control the soil properties (for better plant growth). Doing that on a large scale becomes difficult, especially if you don't wish to use the entire land for growing plants.

In order to set up a raised bed, place a wooden frame, preferably made of wood that doesn't rot quickly, on the ground. Fill the frame with soil (6–12-inch depth is ideal) suitable for growing the kind of plants you are interested in. The size of the frame will depend on the size of the garden. However, they should be placed at such a distance that they allow you to walk between the raised beds to inspect your plants. In the raised bed, you can add any supplements you need to make a suitable composition for plant growth. You can use cocopeat if the soil is very clayey or mix compost if it's devoid of organic matter. You can refer to Chapter 1 on what supplements to use for different soil types. Raised beds can be set up on a terrace as well, but the concrete base should be first waterproofed in order to avoid dampness and long-term deterioration of the building roof.

For people like me who live in smaller spaces with only a balcony, a patio or just a window, you can grow flowers in pots as well. However, you don't have to restrict yourself to boring terracotta or plastic pots. To complement the colourful flowers, you can use your creativity and make pots out of junk lying in your store room. An old copper pot, rustic wooden barrel, a milk can, water drums, rain boots—basically anything that can hold soil can be used to grow plants. For drainage, make a few holes at the bottom, and in case you can't do that, make artificial drainage available in those pots.

In order to arrange for an artificial drainage, you have to create a soil profile inside the container. Set an inch of fine gravel at the base, topped by a coarse gravel layer (at least an inch deep), a layer of sand (at least two inches deep), a layer of charcoal (an inch deep) and then a 5–6-inch-deep layer of actual soil to grow the plant. By introducing these layers, you give space for the water from main soil to run out and collect at the bottom of the pot where there is no hole for it to escape. The gravel layers will retain the water in their air pockets, sand will allow quick drainage of water along with giving support for the roots to grow when they grow from the main soil and charcoal will help remove excess moisture. However, this system does fail in some time because the fine particles of soil will slowly collect at the base of the gravel layer together with moving water. So, if you are going to grow flowers in a DIY pot with no drainage holes, I recommend sticking to annual flowers only. But wait—what are 'annual' flowers?

Classification

Plants, depending on when they flower and how long they live, are broadly put into three categories: annuals, biennials and perennials. This classification is important for plants that depend on the flowering phase to grow their babies—this is why we didn't talk about it in the chapter on foliage plants as they can grow from cuttings.

Annuals

These are plants that complete their life cycle in one season (generally this season lasts for 3–5 months), which means that the time between the seed germination stage and death will only be a few months. They are also often referred to as 'seasonals' as they live for only a season. Seasonal flowers are majorly found growing during spring when the temperature is between 20–30°C. I must point out that the spring temperatures and months also vary across the globe. Within India, in central parts like Maharashtra, spring is warmer with 25–30°C, while northern India is still cool under 20°C at that time. Geographically, the months of spring can also vary. In the Indian subcontinent, spring lasts between the months of February to April, while in colder parts of the world such as in Europe and North America, spring happens between the months of March and May. Whichever month spring falls in in your region, it is during this time of the year when you would find the highest diversity of colourful flowers. Post winters, as the temperatures start to warm up but are still under the peak heat of 30°C or more, longer daylight helps in the blooming of plants. Some popular spring annuals that you may find round the year are pansies, sunflowers, dog flowers and marigolds.

Most annuals need to be started from their seeds and need to be planned in advance so that they reach the appropriate size as the blooming season arrives. For example, seeds for dog flowers are sown and prepared by November-December so that they may reach maturity to

bloom as February-March arrives, as otherwise the plant will miss the appropriate combination of temperature and sun availability that spring provides.

#FUNFACT: *Mughal Gardens in the Indian national capital, which are a part of the Rashtrapati Bhawan (President's House) complex, have absolutely mesmerizing flowers on display in the 15-acre arena. If you get a chance to visit Delhi around that time, you must visit when the gardens are open to the general public during the spring months. This time is called 'Udyanotsav', which means 'festival of gardens'.*

Perennials

Plants that live for multiple seasons and might bloom multiple times are called perennials. Some common examples of perennials that you might have seen around you are *chandni* (crepe jasmine), mogra (scented jasmine), hibiscus, plumeria, adenium, etc. Once started either from a seed or from a cutting, these plants need not be started again and again. In some regions with extreme temperatures, gardeners may start a perennial every year. This is done in places where the climate is extremely cold or extremely hot as a result of which plants are unable to sustain themselves in these extremities. In India, for example, dahlias are often grown as annuals because they are unable to sustain the extreme heat of the tropical country. However, technically speaking, this plant is a perennial as it continues to flower and grow for multiple years.

Most perennials can be grown both vegetatively, i.e., from a cutting (see Chapter 1 for more details) or from a seed.

Biennials

As the name suggests, plants that take two growing seasons to complete their life cycle are called biennials. Such plants are seen to first invest in their vegetative growth, i.e., their roots, stem, branches and leaves, for one growing season, after which they start blooming in the second season. Since there are not a lot of biennials that are grown for their flowers, we will not include biennials in the plants discussed below. Most biennials that flower are of the utility kind, grown only for their seeds, such as onions, carrots, cabbage, etc. We feed on the vegetative part of these plants which only grow for one season. If you let them grow for another season after reaching their full size, they will send out flowers which, after getting pollinated, will give you seeds. However, that will be a distraction here. We are looking at the ornamental kind in this chapter, so we will exclude biennials and focus on perennials and annuals.

Category	Annuals	Biennials	Perennials
Life	Grow, flower, die in one season. They complete their life cycle within a year.	Grow vegetative parts like the stem and leaves in the first season and grow flowers in the second. They complete their life cycle in two seasons.	Live for multiple years
Flowering	Once in their lifetime	Once in their lifetime	Multiple times (some flower only in a certain season while some flower round the year)
Few examples	Daisy, gerbera, dog flower, sunflower	Carrot, cabbage, onion	Hibiscus, hydrangea, bougainvillea, rose

Before I proceed to introduce the different flowers and start listing out their details, a word on their real significance beyond their aesthetic value.

Have you ever wondered why plants flower? It is to produce more babies. But how? These delicate, colourful-looking flowers bear the plant's male and female parts. Some plants bear both the male and female parts in the same flower whereas others bear them separately in different flowers. Since these plants cannot move or walk to transfer the pollen (powder-like thing that comes from the male parts) to the ovaries (female part that will bear the ovules), they have colourful and scented flowers that will attract a bird, a butterfly or a bat to make this transfer happen. This process of transfer from male to female is called pollination, and the agents aiding this process are called the pollinators. When a successful pollination happens, a seed is born that will germinate and help carry forward more generations of that plant.

#FUNFACT: *Flowers are pollinated through agents referred to as 'pollinators'. You may often find them in your garden or balcony. These pollinators have a mutualistic relationship with the flowers whereby both benefit from each other. While the pollinator can get food, find a mate or even shelter in a flower, the flower gets pollinated by that pollinator's movement within a flower and between flowers.*

If you step out on to a balcony or a garden with flowers, there is a good chance to spot a bee, a moth or a bird sucking out food/nectar from a flower, and at night you might also spot a bat doing the same. Like others, bats also visit plants for fruits, nectar and pollen. Interestingly, some plants have over time become so comfortable (read 'evolved') with their pollinator that they won't be able to generate successive generations (read 'seeds') without that pollinator. A common example of this is the relationship between bats and the flowers of an African tree called calabash. The structure of the calabash's flower is such that it needs bats to mediate the pollination, failing which it won't be pollinated naturally. Now imagine, if we lose bats due to forest fragmentation or forest-size reduction, we will also lose the calabash plant.

Interestingly, these flowers also offer what my economist husband would call a 'positive externality'. When pollinators visit a particular flower, it doesn't just help the plant that bears the flower but also the garden as a whole. This is why flowers have become an intrinsic part of planning a garden. Not only do they have an aesthetic value, but they also bear a functional value to the ecosystem. The three flowers that top my list for attracting pollinators to any garden are marigolds, sunflowers and zinnia. They will attract some common bees that will help in pollination, especially in edible plants that you grow for their fruits such as tomatoes, chillies, capsicums, etc. We will talk more about this in the following chapter.

General Care

 Sun

For growing flowers, the most important thing is direct sunlight. If you go back to Chapter 1, you will see that I talked about how only direct sunlight has a good dose of the red part of the spectrum; artificial light sources, like the tube light or bulb, not so much. This red light is key in helping the plants flower and fruit. Therefore, for most flowering plants, you will need a good natural-light area. From our in-depth discussion on what is indoor and outdoor, I am sure that you will by now understand why I refrain from calling any plant 'outdoor' or 'indoor'. It completely depends on where you can provide the necessary conditions for that plant to grow. Since flowering plants necessarily need a good dose of sunlight, you can use a brightly lit south-facing window in your living room as well to grow potted flowers indoors. You may use the windowsill to keep the potted plants or plant them in hanging wooden box planters. My personal choice of wood for planters is acacia and pine. Acacia is readily available in the Indian subcontinent, and you can buy acacia panels and boards in almost any hardware store. On the other hand, pine can be difficult to find. With my experience of designing and making pinewood products for my Garden Up store, I have found that you can buy pine easily in port cities like Mumbai and Surat. Shipping containers carry imported expensive home appliances in pine boxes. Wood from these boxes is sold to the local wood depots from where you can buy pinewood by kilogram and recycle the wood instead of getting a new acacia tree killed for a home-gardening project.

If you are wondering why pine is difficult to find, that's because it grows in high altitudes. It is relatively much easily available in cold regions or temperate countries. Since we primarily lie in the tropical region, pine does not grow that commonly here.

This brings me to the significance of temperature in growing plants, specifically for flowers.

🌡 Temperature

If you recall our discussion on foliage plants, I highlighted how most of them are tropical plants, which is why temperature regulation for them in India won't bother you much. However, for flowers, temperature is a key factor. If a plant does not get the required

amount of cold or warmth—the threshold temperature it needs—it won't flower, and sometimes the seed will not germinate. For example, lavender seeds need a cold treatment to leave dormancy and germinate, a process which is called cold stratification. This process involves sowing seeds in soil, keeping them in low temperature for 10–15 days and then moving them to a hot space. So, in tropical areas like India, lavender is first started in a cold greenhouse and then moved outdoors.

In fact, the sensitivity to temperature is so significant that research shows that day-to-night temperature fluctuation can determine the opening and closing of flowers.

Whenever you buy a flowering plant, be sure of what temperatures it does best in. In most cases, local nurseries will be selling flowers that do well in your area, but when you buy seeds to start a plant, you will have to be mindful of what temperature it will sustain itself in.

🍴 Fertilizer
The third factor that aids in good blooming is a good fertilizer. If a plant is nutrient deprived, preparing for reproduction will be extremely stressful because it is energy consuming for the plant. Therefore, you need to keep your plant well nourished, especially with nitrogen and phosphorus-rich fertilizers. An NPK fertilizer will of course work, and so will the homemade compost. For an extra dose of phosphorus—something that is found to be extremely important in initiating plant flowering—

you can use a powdered form of steamed fish bone meal as well. It's an organic fertilizer that can compensate for the phosphorus that might be lacking in compost. Homemade compost is super rich in nitrogen because of the food that it is made from, but sometimes may lack sufficient phosphorus. Fish bone meal can make up for that. Flowering plants fall in the category of 'medium-heavy feeders'. For any flowering plant, include a good dose of fertilizer at the beginning in the potting mix and keep adding top-up doses every 2–3 months. Further, if you forget to add the feeder, at least make sure that your plant receives a good dose before the flowering season.

Soil

For any kind of flowering plant, you can use a regular potting mix with compost, cocopeat and garden soil in equal proportions. However, some flowers, like magnolias, ageratum, rhododendron, etc., prefer slightly acidic soil that helps in better blooming. To make soil naturally acidic, you can add more organic matter to the soil like cattle manure or even coffee grounds.

Deadheading and Pruning

Another trick that can significantly promote flowering is 'deadheading'. As the name suggests, it's a method to remove dead flower heads. Pinch off the drying flower bud at the point where it is attached to the stem. See the illustration below. The logic behind this is purely ecological, and by now you might have guessed how much I love explaining them! As we know, a flower is the plant's reproductive part that is supposed to reproduce

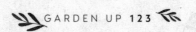

seeds. Ideally, a flower blooms for a certain duration, a month, a week or even just for a few days, after which it dries up. In case that flower was pollinated, the plant would now start investing energy in the next phase of reproduction, i.e., seed production. However, unless you are growing flowers for seeds, by removing the drying flower you are saving the plant energy that it would deploy in seed generation and redirecting it for the production of more flowers instead. Deadheading is a practical and easy method to follow to ensure continuous blooming on your plants. You can practice deadheading on any kind of flowering plant, and it will work like magic.

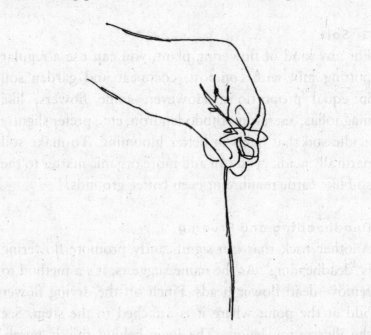

◇ Watering
The watering mantra for flowers remains the same as for any plant—it depends on the plant's natural habitat.

Rainfall varies across areas in frequency and quantity. Remember to always find out if the plant you are buying is water-loving or water-fearing.

Issues You May Face

Symptom: Leaf yellowing in spots

Cause: Could be spider mites, mealybugs or any other insect colonizing the plant and making it weak.

Cure: For terrace or balcony gardeners, this can be a huge problem because the proximity between plants encourages quick growth of the colonizing insects. Use neem oil spray (always remember to read the label for usage) to deal with the pests. If there are just mealybugs on the plant, you can use a simple soap solution as well. Dilute liquid soap (2–3ml in 500 ml water) and spray on affected parts of the plant. You can also mix 5–10 ml of neem oil in the solution if the infestation is heavy.

Symptom: Drying of the plant, starting from the leaves

Cause: The logic behind drying is the same for any plant, flowering or not—it is watering issues.

In case the plant is left underwater for several days, it will dry up, and bringing it back to life will be challenging. However, getting the watering right is among the easier problems to solve.

Cure: If you are not sure how to water a given plant, observe it. See how many days or hours it takes for its stems and leaves to get droopy. And when you do water, do so thoroughly. This will tell you the frequency of watering you need for that particular plant, saving you from both under as well as overwatering.

Symptom: No flowering or few flowers

Cause: It could lack enough sun, enough nutrients or it might be because of general dormancy.

Cure: Every flowering plant should get at least 4–5 hours of direct sunlight. Of course, the temperature needed could be different. For example, both mogra as well as pansies like minimum 5–6 hours of direct sunlight, but mogra likes temperatures of 25°C or above whereas pansies prefer <25°C. If the sunlight needs are taken care of and the plant is still not flowering well, add a phosphorus-rich fertilizer. Lastly, even if the fertilizer does not help, try giving a deep pruning to your plant before its flowering season. This will help in breaking the plant out of its dormant state.

Symptom: Ants

Cause: Honeydew (a sugary secretion for the plants)

Cure: Ants live in a close relationship with soft-bodied insects like mealybugs that puncture the plant to release the honeydew. In return, ants provide protection to these soft-bodied insects from other insects. A temporary solution is to attack the ants with a commercial ant spray (some sprays are very concentrated and can also kill the plant, so spray it only around the pot, avoiding the plant), but a more permanent solution is to make your plant less susceptible to mealybugs. That can happen when you keep a close eye on watering. An irregularly-watered plant that is under stress falls prey to mealybugs more often. Further, you can hang sticky mats for monitoring insects visiting your garden. This way you will have a head start on an upcoming insect infestation, and you can take precautionary measures, like spraying the plant with neem solution.

Symptom: Black and/or white spots on the leaves and sometimes on flowers

---

Cause: Fungal attack/rot

Cure: Plants standing in constantly moist soil are prone to fungal attacks. As a temporary fix, you can use a copper-based fungicide powder. However, in order to deal with this situation more permanently, allow water to dry out between waterings, and if you are growing a plant that loves wet feet, use a well-draining potting mix that does not hold water for long.

Plants You Can Grow

Here is a list of flowering plants one can grow seasonally as well as around the year, arranged in order of ease of growing.

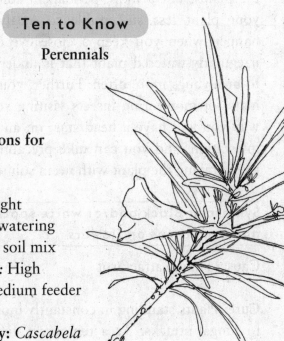

Ten to Know

Perennials

1. Kaner

Suitable Conditions for Good Growth

- ☀ *Sun:* Bright light
- 🪣 *Water:* Low watering
- 🌱 *Soil:* Regular soil mix
- 🌡 *Temperature:* High
- 🍴 *Fertilizer:* Medium feeder

Common Variety: *Cascabela thevetia*, available commonly in yellow, white and pink colours.

Grow For

- Ease of care: The waxy coating on the leaves is an adaptation of the plant to sustain itself in low water areas. This plant is also very tolerant to high temperatures, making it super easy to grow without much care.

Common Issues

- Toxicity: It is a highly toxic plant if consumed. Merely keeping it in your house will not hurt anyone, but keep it away from the reach of children and pets, who might try to eat the leaves.

Propagation: Cutting with rooting hormone method. Try to take a cutting of 5–6 inches in length at least.

Super Tip: Rooting of hard stem cutting such as kaner is difficult. In order to ensure better success, first use a sharp, clean knife that enables you to make a clean cut with no microbial infection. Second, don't remove the cutting from the soil for at least 2–3 months. If the stem is disturbed without root formation, repotting will not help, and you will have to start from scratch again. A way to know whether the cutting will survive and whether or not your efforts have succeeded is by looking out for new leaves. Fresh growth is a sign that the cutting is forming a root system that is bringing in enough water and nutrients to sprout out new leaves.

2. Ixora

Suitable Conditions for Good Growth

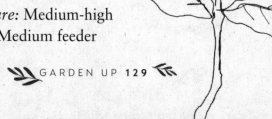

- ☀ *Sun:* Bright-medium light
- ◇ *Water:* Medium watering
- ✎ *Soil:* Regular soil mix
- 🌡 *Temperature:* Medium-high
- 🍴 *Fertilizer:* Medium feeder

Common Varieties: There over 500 species of ixora, but two common ones that can be grown easily are jungle geranium (*Ixora coccinea*) and Chinese ixora (*Ixora chinensis*).

Grow For
- Aesthetics: Flowers bloom in large clusters in deep colours of pink, red and yellow, making it ideal for any garden.

Common Issues
- Intolerance to low temperatures. Ixora cannot withstand low temperatures (<20°C), in which case you can grow them as an annual, meaning that you start a new plant every year at least two months before the spring. In case you stay in a tropical place with temperatures of 20–35°C, you will find this plant flowering round the year as a perennial.

Propagation: Cutting with rooting hormone.

Super Tip: Since ixora is tolerant to partial shade as well, you can bring this plant indoors and place it next to the window to add colour in your living room.

3. Peacock Flower

Suitable Conditions for Good Growth

☼ *Sun:* Bright light
🪣 *Water:* Medium watering
🪴 *Soil:* Regular soil mix
🌡 *Temperature:* High
🍴 *Fertilizer:* Medium feeder

Common Variety: *Caesalpinia pulcherrima*

Grow For

• Aesthetics: Peacock flowers can grow up to 3 metres and can be used to add some height in the garden.

Common Issues: Spider mites

Propagation: Start from a seed.

Super Tip: Grow the plant in a cluster, especially if you have a garden. This also attracts hummingbirds to visit the flower.

4. Plumeria

Suitable Conditions for Good Growth

☀ *Sun:* Bright light
💧 *Water:* Medium watering
🪴 *Soil:* Regular potting mix
🌡 *Temperature:* High-medium
🍴 *Fertilizer:* Medium feeder

Common Variety: Champa/frangipani (*Plumeria obtusa* and *Plumeria rubra*)

Grow For

- Treat to your senses: Plumeria is not only an attractive flowering plant with large white flowers and waxy coated leaves, but it is also a very fragrant plant.

Common Issues: Intolerance to overwatering

Propagation: Cutting with rooting hormone method. However, if you don't have access to rooting hormone, you can still try planting the cutting in soil to initiate root formation (choose a stem that's neither too thick nor too thin, about 2–3 cm thick and 3–4 inches long. To avoid the rotting/decay of such a cutting, let it dry from the base for a couple of days before dipping in rooting hormone and planting in soil.

Super Tip: If you are not looking to grow a jungle but to have only one perfect plant to give a tropical feel to your balcony or terrace, grow plumeria. If grown in a large (>20-inch) pot, it can quickly grow to 5 ft or larger. Its leaves are broad, matte green with a very prominent vein structure. Additionally, the flowers are large and fragrant. The plant can continue blooming in warm climates around the year.

#FUNFACT: *Plumeria flowers don't hold any nectar, but the sweet fragrance of the flowers at night confuses the moths that visit the plant as they associate the smell with the nectar. Although they do not find any nectar, they end up helping in the pollination of the flowers and helping the plumeria blossom from seeds.*

5. Crepe Jasmine

Suitable Conditions for Good Growth

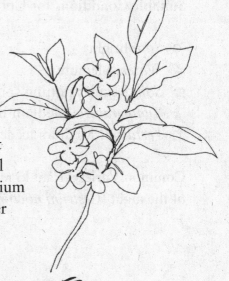

☀ *Sun:* Bright light
💧 *Water:* Medium-wet feet
🪴 *Soil:* Regular potting soil
🌡 *Temperature:* High-medium
🍴 *Fertilizer:* Medium feeder

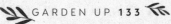

Common Variety: Chandni (*Tabernaemontana divaricata*)

Grow For
- Aesthetics: The milky white, pinwheel-shaped flower is a treat to the eyes. Even if the flowers are not blooming, the bush will remain evergreen if cared for appropriately.

Common Issues
- Drying of the plant/intolerance to underwatering

Propagation: Stem cutting with rooting hormone

Super Tip: For a tall and bushy chandni, try not to let the soil dry completely. It prefers moist soil at all times. This will help the plant to grow steadily.

6. Night Blooming Jasmine

Suitable Conditions for Good Growth

☼ *Sun:* Bright
🏷 *Water:* Medium
🪴 *Soil:* Regular potting soil
🌡 *Temperature:* Medium-high
🍴 *Fertilizer:* Medium feeder

Common Variety: Raat ki rani/lady of the night (*Cestrum nocturnum*)

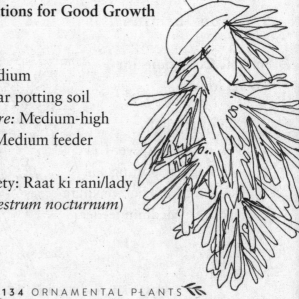

Grow For

- Scent and aesthetics: As the name suggests, this one blooms at night with a strong smell, and before the sun rises, the flowers dislodge from the stem. The flowers have a short life of one night, but the fragrance makes them worth it. You can collect the fallen flowers the next morning and place them in different corners of the house. The fallen flowers also retain the scent for several hours.

Common Issues

- Rare drooping or drying of leaves: Most perennials that I am sharing here are hardy plants that can sustain extreme hot and cold temperatures. The only thing that can deeply upset them is regular watering issues. Both underwatering and overwatering can dry up the plant or cause leaves to yellow. For absolute beginners, I recommend touching the soil to see if it sticks to your finger or not. If soil does not stick to your finger while taking out a pinch of soil from the topsoil layer, only then add water and ensure that you are not letting the soil dry out completely between waterings. If the potting mix has high clay content, the topsoil might start developing cracks upon drying, but that doesn't necessarily mean that the soil is dry. Taking out a pinch of soil from underneath will help understand the moisture level better.

Propagation: Stem cutting with rooting hormone method

Super Tip: In extreme hot weather, especially if you stay in a place where local summer winds (loo) are common, keep the plant guarded from the intense winds. The trick you can use is to start the plant beside a wall or a tree that will act as a barrier to hot winds, as otherwise the plant will start curling up and shedding its leaves during June-July summers.

7. Mogra

Suitable Conditions for Good Growth

☼ *Sun:* Bright-medium
💧 *Water:* Medium
🌱 *Soil:* Regular potting soil
🌡 *Temperature:* Medium-high
🍴 *Fertilizer:* Medium feeder

Common Variety: Mogra/Arabian Jasmine (*Jasminum sambac*)

Grow For: Low maintenance and scent

Common Issues: No flowering. Generally, improving light availability and fertilization helps in fostering flowering.

Propagation: Stem cutting with rooting hormone method

Super Tip: Use loose and compost-rich soil to grow Arabian jasmine for good growth. Instead of compost, if you find cow manure, use that for good flowering.

8. Hibiscus

Suitable Conditions for Good Growth

☀ *Sun:* Bright
✍ *Water:* Medium
🧴 *Soil:* Regular potting soil
🌡 *Temperature:* High
🍴 *Fertilizer:* Medium feeder

Common Varieties: *Hibiscus syriacus*, *Hibiscus rosa-sinensis* and *Hibiscus sabdariffa*

Grow For
- Aesthetics: Use for a spark of red colour amidst the greenery of your plants. However, there are other colour options as well, such as yellow and pink.
- Medicinal properties: Hibiscus tea is rich in vitamin C and has been recommended for patients suffering from high blood pressure and diabetes for its medicinal properties.

Common Issues
- Insects: This plant is a mealybug magnet.

Propagation: Stem cutting with rooting hormone

Super Tip: Hibiscus is great for herbal tea. Boil 3–4 flowers in a litre of water and add 3 tablespoons of lemon juice. Let the tea steep for 10–15 minutes and serve hot or cold. It will have a very calming smell and mild taste. Since there are a large variety of hibiscus plants available in the market, *Hibiscus sabdariffa* is the recommended species for tea-making purposes.

9. Bougainvillea

Suitable Conditions for Good Growth

☀ *Sun:* Bright
🪣 *Water:* Low
🌱 *Soil:* Regular potting soil
🌡 *Temperature:* High
🍴 *Fertilizer:* Medium feeder

Common Varieties: This plant is available in a variety of colours and species. My top three suggestions for this plant are *Bougainvillea glabra*, *Bougainvillea peruviana* and *Bougainvillea × buttiana* (it is a hybrid between glabra and peruviana).

Grow For
- Aesthetics and low maintenance: A full-bloom bougainvillea against a white wall is a treat for the eyes. Grow them for their colour and easy care.

Common Issues: No flowering and low tolerance to overwatering

Propagation: Stem cutting with rooting hormone method.

Super Tip: Prune the plant before spring and add a trellis for support. You can also allow the plant to climb a boundary wall. When the flowers come out, it will look gorgeous.

#FUNFACT: *Any gardener would often come across terms such as 'hybrid' and 'heirloom' while buying seeds. What they really signify is the origin of that plant's seed. 'Heirloom' varieties are native varieties that occur in a particular region/area for several years and are known to best suit the climate there. In Hindi, you can come across a term for heirloom that is 'desi'. It's not only limited to plants, but also used for cattle. For example, 'Gir cow' is native or 'desi' to Gir (a small area in the western state of India, Gujarat). Likewise, the emmer wheat variety—khapli gehu which is the parent of the modern day wheat grown in India—is a heirloom variety that grows well in Maharashtra. However, the common varieties that are popularly used now are the hybrid kind, whereby different heirloom varieties are crossed to retain the best quality of the plant. For example, Sonalika, first developed in 1963 in Mexico, is a very high yield wheat variety with disease-resistant properties and is popularly grown in different parts of India. The debate over which kind of seed is better, hybrid or heirloom, is beyond the scope of this book. I, by no means, want to recommend any particular kind for home gardeners. In my garden, I use a mix of heirloom and hybrid—honestly, whatever I can get my hands on.*

10. Rose

Suitable Conditions for Good Growth

- ☼ *Sun:* Bright
- 💧 *Water:* Low
- 🪴 *Soil:* Regular potting soil
- 🌡 *Temperature:* Low-medium
- 🍴 *Fertilizer:* Medium-heavy feeder (once every 2–3 months)

Common Varieties: There are several varieties you can find, especially the hybrid kinds. My top five favourites are hybrid tea rose (*Rosa hybrid*), floribunda rose (*Rosa floribunda)*, Kashmiri rose (*Rosa* 'Kashmir'), alba rose (*Rosa alba*) and grandiflora rose (*Rosa grandiflora*). Within each of the rose species mentioned above, there are additional subspecies. These subspecies vary from each other primarily in colour. The care for them, however, largely remains the same.

Grow For

- Fragrance: The fragrance of a flower is a signal for the pollinators to attract them. Different kinds of chemicals that contribute to the fragrance have been extracted for several decades in modern times to use in perfumery. You can also just bring in the potted plant for the scent in your living space.
- Medicinal properties: Rose is known to soothe skin, prevent infections and heal scars, among its many other medicinal benefits.

Common Issues

- Black spots: *Diplocarpon rosae* is a common fungus that grows on rose stems and leaves, causing dark patches or spots. With continued infestation, the plant will also become weak and start shedding leaves. Additionally, once the plant is under the fungal infection for long, it makes it prone to more infections. It is better to treat the fungus at an early stage. If you are noticing the infection on only a leaf or two, clip them. Do not, however, leave them in the ground, but preferably dispose of the infected leaves away from the plant. If the infection has spread to multiple leaves, use a fungicidal spray or a powder. There are both chemical-based or organic fungicides available. Post treatment also ensure that the plant is not getting excessive water. Moist conditions promote fungal growth.

- With rose, you may also face other issues like less flowering, slow growth and drying of leaves.

Propagation: Stem cutting with rooting hormone

Super Tip: Covering the soil under the rose plant with mulch will help reduce infections in rose plants. For mulching, you can use dried leaves, hay, cardboard pieces and even newspaper in shredded form.

Perennial flowers shared above are plants that ideally should live for multiple seasons. However, depending on the weather conditions in your area, most of them can also be treated as seasonals, where you can plan them in advance in such a way that by the flowering season, these plants have reached the optimum size. However, plants that grow as a bush (e.g., bougainvillea) are not ideal for growing as a seasonal plant. It is a woody shrub that will take multiple seasons to grow a few feet. For regions with extreme cold weather where through most of the year temperatures remain under 20°C, you can focus on growing annuals. However, in regions where it is mostly hot with temperatures remaining above 30°C round the year, you can invest more of your effort in growing perennials.

1. Marigold

Suitable Conditions for Good Growth

☀ *Sun:* Bright sun

💧 *Water:* Medium

🪨 *Soil:* Regular potting mix

🌡 *Temperature:* Medium

🍴 *Fertilizer:* Low (only before flowering sets in)

Common Varieties: Mexican marigold (*Tagetes erecta),* seasonal variety. In recent times, perennial species of marigold have also gained popularity. However, my experience with growing the *Tagetes erecta*, a seasonal kind of marigold, has been the best. It can be started in the month of November for northern states of India, such as Haryana, Punjab, Delhi, Uttar Pradesh, as well as the entirety of central, north-eastern and south India. For areas with heavy snow in January, such as Himachal Pradesh, Jammu and Kashmir and parts of Uttarakhand, seasonal marigolds can be started indoors in December and then moved outdoors during the spring.

Grow For: Aesthetics, pollinators and keeping mosquitoes away

Common Issues: No or few flowers and drying of the plant

Propagation: Start from seeds.

Super Tip: Marigolds are great companion plants that should be grown with cabbage, broccoli, tomatoes, potatoes and squash in a vegetable garden.

2. Indian Cress

Suitable Conditions for Good Growth

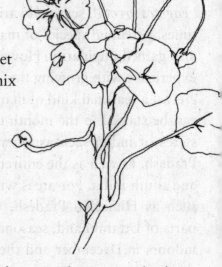

☀ *Sun:* Bright sun
💧 *Water:* Medium-wet feet
🪴 *Soil:* Regular potting mix
🌡 *Temperature:* Medium
🍴 *Fertilizer:* Low

Common Variety:
Nasturtium/Indian cress
(*Tropaeolum majus*)

Grow For
- Aesthetics and ease of care: They grow both as climbing and bushy plants that need minimal

attention. In fact, some gardeners like to refer to them as the ones that 'thrive on neglect'.

Common Issues

- Less flowers: They generally don't end up with problems, but heavy feeding with fertilizer can lead to lush green growth with no flowers. Keep the soil well-drained and use old, decomposed compost only for fertilizing. I like to add fertilizer to them around February by using a handful of compost.

Propagation: Start from tubers. Plant in late winter to get them to bloom in spring season.

Super Tip: Grow these plants for keeping control on aphids. This will reduce the effort and time spent on pesticide use. Additionally, you will have brilliant bright colours in your garden.

3. Mexican Sunflower

Suitable Conditions for Good Growth

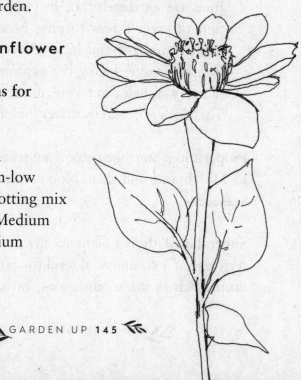

☼ *Sun:* Bright sun
🖐 *Water:* Medium-low
🪴 *Soil:* Regular potting mix
🌡 *Temperature:* Medium
🍴 *Fertilizer:* Medium

Common Variety: Some varieties of this plant are also perennials. Among the annuals, try the *Tithonia rotundifolia*.

Grow For

- Tall flowering plant with low maintenance: There are very few seasonals that can quickly grow to be a few metres in height and are still not very demanding in terms of their needs. Among the over fifty varieties of tithonia, some can even reach 5 metres or more in height.
- This plant does not demand a very high quality of life. It can sustain itself in both overwatered and underwatered soil and doesn't mind neglect at all.

Common Issues

- Leaves turning brown: If the months from April–June are extremely hot in your region, you might find tithonia leaves turning brown because of the intense sunlight and heat. Of course, changing the location and reducing the exposure to the troubling factor will help, but you can also ignore the plant. This does not heavily affect the plant's blooming.

Propagation: Start the plant from seeds between February to March and find them blooming in the early summer season.

Super Tip: Tithonia plant species are used as an organic fertilizer at a commercial level for farmers growing cash crops such as maize, tomatoes, carrots, etc. At a home garden level, you can use the dried-out plant after its flowering season as mulch to cover the soil. Mulching cuts off the contact of the plant above ground from the soil. This reduces the insects and diseases in the plant and also reduces moisture loss and heat loss from soil, thereby helping in better growth.

4. Nigella Plant

Suitable Conditions for Good Growth

☀ *Sun:* Bright sun
🖌 *Water:* Medium-wet feet
🌱 *Soil:* Regular potting mix
🌡 *Temperature:* Medium-low
🍴 *Fertilizer:* Medium

Common Variety: Devil in the bush/nigella plant (*Nigella damascena*)

Grow For
- Aesthetics: This one brings out flowers in shades of blue—from a dull blue to a bright lavender colour.

Common Issues
- Quick death at seedling stage.
- Most flowers started from seeds are sown in seedling trays and then transferred to bigger pots. However, some plants such as the nigella plant can be very sensitive to that transfer. For such kinds, sow the

seeds directly in large pots by spreading the seeds 2–3 cm apart and buried an inch deep.

Propagation: Start from seeds.

Super Tip: Gardeners love to use this devil in the bush as a filler plant, i.e., to fill vacant spaces in landscape arrangements.

5. Dog Flower

Suitable Conditions for Good Growth

☼ *Sun:* Bright sun
⬧ *Water:* Medium-wet feet
🗫 *Soil:* Regular potting mix
🌡 *Temperature:* Medium
🍴 *Fertilizer:* Medium

Common Variety: Traditionally grown as an annual in India, this plant is actually a short-lived perennial. I preferred to keep it in my list because of the popularity of this plant. As children, we used to love playing with its flowers in school because of its fascinating design, resembling a dog's face. Some also refer to it as the snapdragon plant (*Antirrhinum majus*).

Grow For

- Aesthetics: They are extremely popular in flower bouquet arrangements. You can make DIY flower arrangements for your own home or for friends and family by arranging a bunch of snapdragon stems together.

Common Issues

- Infections and diseases: Avoid overhead watering of this plant. It only enjoys being watered at the roots directly, and this reduces the pest and infection problems. Try to tackle an infection at the earliest. Snapdragons also get blight very often, in which case use a copper-based fungicide to stop the disease from spreading. Also remember to physically remove the affected parts.

Propagation: Start from stem cutting with rooting hormone method. Use a 2-inch-long stem for the cutting. Plant in late winter in order to get them to bloom in the spring season.

Super Tip: In order to encourage the growth of more flowers on the plant, constantly remove any side growing stem with a sharp pruner or a scissor.

6. Pansy

Suitable Conditions for Good Growth

☀ *Sun:* Bright

💧 *Water:* Medium

🪱 *Soil:* Regular potting mix rich in organic matter (use compost or vermicompost instead of chemical fertilizer to increase organic matter in soil)

🌡 *Temperature:* Medium-low

🍴 *Fertilizer:* Heavy feeder. Once the plant sapling has five or six leaves, add a handful of good-quality manure or compost per pot)

Common Variety: Pansy (*Viola tricolor*)

Grow For: Aesthetics

Common Issues

- Fungal issues: Pansies are prone to powdery mildew, blight and cercospora leaf spot. All of them cause different kinds of spots on the plants, thereby affecting their aesthetic charm.

Propagation: Start from seeds in September. You can also buy a sapling in early autumn (October).

Super Tip: Pansies are probably among the most favourite edible flowers for chefs. You can find them in salads, tea infusions and dessert toppings, to name a few. If you wish to include them in your home cooking, ensure that you aren't using the pesticide-treated pansies.

7. Sunflower

Suitable Conditions for Good Growth

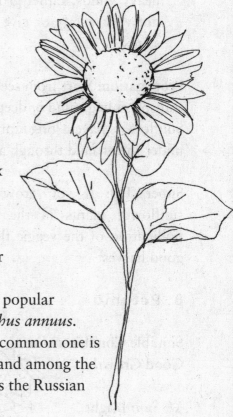

☀ *Sun:* Bright
💧 *Water:* Medium
🪴 *Soil:* Regular potting mix (rich in organic matter and slightly acidic type)
🌡 *Temperature:* Medium
🍴 *Fertilizer:* Medium feeder

Common Variety: The most popular Sunflower species is *Helianthus annuus*. Among the dwarf variety, a common one is suntastic yellow sunflower, and among the tall variety, a common one is the Russian mammoth sunflower.

Grow For
- Pollinators and oil: Sunflower is a cash crop which is grown on a large scale for oil from its seeds. The large flower also appeals to the bees.

Common Issues

- Collapsing of the plant: Since sunflowers have long delicate stems, they are susceptible to collapsing in heavy winds. Either grow them in an area which is not very windy or give extra support to individual stems.

Propagation: Start from seeds in seedling trays and then transplant in ground or deep pots (at least 14-inch deep). Sunflowers have a long taproot, and they love to expand under the ground through a heavy root network.

Super Tip: If you grow vegetables evenly, spread sunflower plants in the garden to help get more pollination of the veggie flowers and thereby ensure a good harvest.

8. Petunia

Suitable Conditions for Good Growth

☼ *Sun:* Bright

🝆 *Water:* Regular

🪴 *Soil:* Regular potting mix (rich in organic matter)

🌡 *Temperature:* Medium-low

🍴 *Fertilizer:* Medium feeder (feed at the sapling stage and once the first set of flowers emerge)

Common Varieties: *Petunia grandiflora* and *Petunia multiflora*

Grow For
- Aesthetics and long-lasting seasonals: Petunias will last for 5–6 months in mild Indian winters. Add them to your collection for a spark of colour.

Common Issues: Fungal attack

Propagation: Start from seeds, but keep them in semi-shade conditions under the early morning sun or evening sun when they are first starting out.

Super Tip: Grow petunias in hanging baskets. You can recycle the fruit baskets that are traditionally used in Indian homes for gifting in festivals and weddings. Line the basket with a coir lining or agricultural fabric. Add well-draining organic matter-rich soil to grow petunias.

9. Makhmali Flower

Suitable Conditions for Good Growth

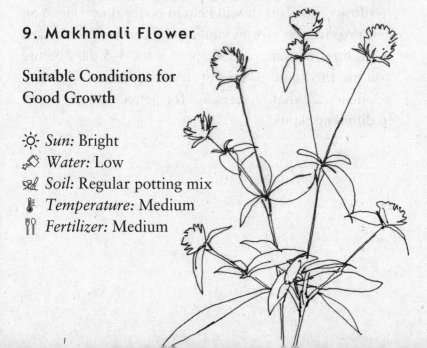

☀ *Sun:* Bright
💧 *Water:* Low
🌱 *Soil:* Regular potting mix
🌡 *Temperature:* Medium
🍴 *Fertilizer:* Medium

Common Varieties: Makhmali, globe amaranth and gomphrena (*Gomphrena globosa*)

Grow For
- Ease of care and disease resistance

Common Issues
- Wilting: Overwatering does not work for makhmali. It is better to keep it underwatered than over-watered, so keep a close watch on how frequently you water this one.

Propagation: Start from seeds, and in case you have one of these plants already, spread the dried flowers in soil. There is a good chance that the naturally-dried flowers would have formed seeds and will germinate in a new pot.

Super Tip: Use mustard cakes dissolved in water for fertilizing the plant. It will help in better flowering. You can prepare the mix by adding 250 grams of mustard in 10 litres of water and keeping it for 4–5 days before you use the liquid to directly fertilize the soil. This is a popular trick that farmers use for better flower growth in different plants.

10. Larkspur

Suitable Conditions for Good Growth

☀ *Sun:* Bright
💧 *Water:* Medium
🔧 *Soil:* Regular potting mix
🌡 *Temperature:* Medium-low
🍴 *Fertilizer:* Medium

Common Variety: Larkspur (*Delphinium majus*)

Grow For
- Aesthetics and ease of care: Use larkspur to create a low maintenance, tall flowering hedge for the autumn season or late summers.

Common Issues
- Fungus and insects: Botrytis blight or grey mould (a fungus) attacks this plant in moist conditions. Therefore, try growing it in warm and dry areas only. Aphids also thrive on these plants, for which you can try introducing their natural predators in the garden such as lady beetles.

Propagation: Start the plant from seeds in September–October or May–June.

Super Tip: To invite butterflies in your garden, larkspur is the perfect plant to grow either in pots or in the ground directly.

Given below is the monthly sowing chart for seasonal flowers. The primary factor considered for this division is temperature and rainfall. However, I do understand that even within these regions, temperature and rainfall may vary greatly. For regional classification based on seasons of India, please refer to page 10.

Plants	Region 1 (Sowing of seeds)	Region 2 (Sowing of seeds)
Flowers		
Dog flower	September–November	September–November
Indian cress	October–November	November–December
Larkspur	September–November	October–December
Makhmali	August–September	September–October
Marigold	August–November	September–November
Mexican sunflower	February–March	January–April
Nigella plant	December–January	December–January
Pansy	September–October	June–September
Petunia	August–October	August–October
Sunflower	December–March	September–October and February–April

Chapter 4
UTILITY PLANTS

Cherry tomatoes for your salad, along with some lettuce and beets, coming right from your personal farm. How does that sound? By the way, this 'personal farm' can be just a windowsill or even acres of land. You can grow anything and everything, anywhere! At first it may seem a little intimidating, but once you have a handle on how it works, how to sow the seeds, how to prepare and how to fix the issues, you can practically be a farmer. I mean it. I believe that nobody is born with a green thumb, but if you have the motivation, you can develop an intuition regarding plant care. Watching how they behave and logically eliminating the factors that cause issues, in a step-by-step process, helps in utilizing the most of whatever space you have.

As a gardening content creator on different social media platforms, such as YouTube, Instagram and Facebook, I have seen interest in home gardening increase dramatically since the pandemic hit us in 2020. One thing that every home gardener, beginner or pro, wanted to do was try their hand at growing food. The pleasure of seeing a tomato from the refrigerator grow into another tomato is priceless. Even if it's a small harvest, the sense of accomplishment it gives is incomparable. What came as a surprise to me was the interest I saw among children (4–16 years old) who wanted to learn more about how their food grows and what it takes to grow a bunch of vegetables.

4.1 EDIBLE PLANTS

In this section, I will break down the complicated world of growing food at a home-garden level in simple steps. The edibles I share here can be both grown in a pot or in the ground as long as the plant is grown in the right-sized pot with adequate amount of the resources it needs. However, before we jump to the 'how to' part of growing edibles, I quickly want to take you through some basics and explain why they matter in growing vegetables.

Seasonals and Annuals

From the last chapter, you have by now grasped that some plants live only for a season (which lasts for a few months) and others for two or more seasons. While growing plants for food, the focus is on which part is the edible kind and how long it may take to grow that. For example, a spinach plant, which may live for multiple seasons, is grown for its leaves, and they taste the best when they are young. So, you harvest all

the leaves when they attain the desired size without regard for the actual lifetime of the plant. Spinach for us is 'seasonal'. On the other hand, plants such as pomegranates are grown for the fruit, and even though the leaves come out quickly, we have to wait for a couple of seasons to get the fruit, which puts it in the annual category.

Starting from Seeds

Most edibles can be started from seeds, especially the seasonal kind. For propagation through seeds, you can sow the seeds in a seedling tray. I am often asked two things at this stage. First, why start in seedling trays? Second, what kind of soil to use to sow seeds? Let me address both.

Seedling Trays

They help in saving time, effort and energy. It is easier to manipulate the temperature and humidity for seed germination (at this point light does not really matter). It is easier to place a lavender seed sown in seedling trays in a refrigerator for cold treatment, but placing a 12-inch pot inside a refrigerator might be actually impossible. Further, in a seedling tray you would know which of the seeds are actually fertile to germinate and worth investing the energy of preparing the soil and setting up the pots. Imagine preparing a 12-inch-big pot to grow okra. You prepare the soil mix, sow the seeds in the pot, find the perfect spot and care for it over the week, only to find out that of all those seeds that you had sown, only one seed actually germinated!

When I say 'seedling trays', you don't necessarily have to buy the typical kind. You can instead get creative and use empty eggshells, egg trays, food-delivery boxes, milk cartons or even cardboard rolls from the toilet paper. As the seed germinates and sprouts out cotyledons, you can carefully move it to a bigger pot or wait for 4–5 true leaves to set in. I wait for the true leaves to set in so that the plant is more hardy and mature to face the real world (a bigger pot or the ground). You can start seeds indoors on a window sill or outdoors. I keep seedling starter pots in a large plastic container with a lid outdoors. The lid reduces the moisture loss, saving the effort of watering the soil every time it dries. Additionally, it also keeps the heat trapped, especially in the evenings as the temperature drops. Hot and moist conditions help in germination for tropical plants, which are the ones that I have primarily talked about in this book. In my balcony, I also have a major pigeon problem, as they are very curious and live to look for insects in the pots. They uproot the seedling, so the box with a cover also protects the plant babies.

At the germination stage, sun is not really important for the seeds. However, once they emerge from the soil, sunlight becomes important. In the absence of enough sun, the seedling becomes tall and lanky as it grows towards the light source looking for light, eventually becoming weak. Once that happens, they can fall on the soil or the water pressure can push them down, and they usually die within a few days. Providing 4–5 hours of sunlight should be enough for any edibles you are starting as seedlings. The reason we are specifically talking about the seedling germination in the edible section of the book is because most other plants discussed before can be started from a cutting or bought as a sapling. However, for growing food, especially on a large scale, one needs to prepare for sowing with proper planning and with the right resources. If your seedlings are not ready at the right time, the entire life cycle of the plant will be delayed.

The flowering and fruit setting is very much dependent on the climate. If the germination is too early or too late, one would not get the right harvest despite all the efforts. For example, in Mumbai, tomatoes do very well in summers. However, unlike in north India, I don't have the liberty to start tomato seeds in June or July. Why? Because the Mumbai monsoon is very intense, and, at times, weeks can go by with absolutely no sun in sight. In the absence of enough sun, tomato seeds, even if they germinate, will not set forth flowers, let alone the expectation of some ripe tomatoes. So, for Mumbai, I should start the seeds any time between December and April to have a decent harvest. However, in north India where it is still quite cold in December–January, one should start the sowing only in February. This can go on until August. Given below is the monthly sowing chart for seasonal edibles for select regions in India. The primary factor considered for this division is temperature and rainfall. However, I do understand that even within these regions temperature and rainfall may vary greatly. For regional classification based on seasons of India, please refer to page 10.

Plants	Region 1 (Sowing of seeds)	Region 2 (Sowing of seeds)
Edibles		
Beetroot	August–September	August–September
Broccoli	August–January	September–October
Coriander	October–November	October–November
Fenugreek	October–November and August–September	October–November and June–July
Gourds	February–June	Round the year, except in the monsoon season (skip June –August)
Iceberg lettuce	September–October	October–December
Okra	February–May	January–April and September–October
White Radish	September–January	September–October
Spinach	January–March, September–November	September–January
Tomato	March–August	July–October, January–May

When you sow the seeds in a seedling pot or tray, start two seeds per pot/cavity. This is done to improve the return on effort-investment. In case both seeds germinate, you can separate the two at the seedling stage before planting them in the larger pot or ground.

Soil for Seedlings

Seeds need soil as a substrate in order to provide the appropriate microclimate to sprout and develop roots. For the earliest days, the baby plant (at the cotyledon stage) has enough nutrients within the seed to sprout. For that reason, you can use a tissue paper or a planting sponge as well. The key to germination is temperature and humidity. Only once the roots emerge and the plant proceeds from the seedling (two-leaf stage) to the sapling

stage (3–5 leaves), it needs external nutrient input. Therefore, I like to start in soil over tissue paper method. The soil should be well draining and nutrient rich. My recommended mix is equal amounts of cocopeat and compost as seed starter mix.

Watering for Seedlings

The frequency of watering, of course, depends on what veggie you are growing, but for the context of this chapter, all the aforementioned edibles like water whenever the top one inch of soil dries out. While watering, also be mindful of the delicate leaves that can get damaged with water pressure and the roots which may also get displaced. I highly recommend a watering instrument that sends out a water shower in sprinkler fashion (see illustration below).

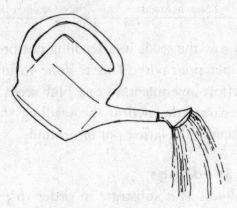

When to Transplant

Theoretically, the job of a seedling tray/pot is to improve the success rate with germination, after which at any time the plant can be removed from the seed starter and placed in the actual pot or ground (wherever you intend to continue growing it.) However, sensitivity of the baby

plant to the new habitat can seriously affect its growth. When the seed has just germinated, it is delicate and can easily succumb to water or heat stress. Therefore, the recommended stage of transplantation is the sapling stage when the baby plant has 4–5 leaves. Additionally, if the sowing was done indoors, before moving the plant outdoors and leaving it there, try to acclimatize it to the outdoor conditions for a few days. Acclimatization is the process of making the plant accustomed to the new temperature, humidity and sun conditions. For this, you can start by moving the plant/sapling outdoors every day for 4–5 hours (preferably not when the sun intensity is the highest or the temperatures are at their most extreme) and then move it back indoors. After repeating this for 3–5 days, you can let the plant grow outdoors, by which time it should have gotten used to the outdoor conditions. A way to judge a successful acclimatization is to closely observe the leaves for the first 24–48 hours. If they start drooping or the plant stem starts collapsing, that indicates that your plant is not ready for the outdoors yet and needs more time to adjust. In this case, you can extend the acclimatizing hours outdoors, but you should move the plant indoors during the afternoon and at nighttime.

Vegetative Propagation Method

Edibles that grow in tree form (mostly fruit trees such as guava, pomegranate, lemon, etc.) can be grown from a cutting. Root formation on this cutting is popularly induced by a method called 'air layering'. Simple water propagation or rooting hormone propagation results in lower success rates for fruit trees.

Air Layering

The motive is to induce rooting under the node area.

a. Select a medium-thick stem (4–5 cm thickness) and remove one inch of the stem skin just under the node using a knife.

b. Scratch the exposed fibrous surface of the stem with the knife.

c. Prepare a small ball (diameter ~5–6 cm) of potting mix with 50% cocopeat and 50% garden soil, 2–3 grams of rooting hormone powder and water (just enough to hold the ball together like a dough ball).

d. Separately dissolve 2–3 grams of rooting hormone powder in 50 ml water and apply this solution over the exposed part of the stem. Further, allow this to dry for 10–15 mins.

e. Over the rooting hormone applied on the stem, wrap the potting mix dough ball prepared with cocopeat, garden soil and rooting hormone. Wrap this with a plastic sheet tried with thread as shown below.

f. In a month, the exposed area will develop roots and can be detached from the mother plant. In the 30 days before detachment, you can open the plastic wrapper (at 10-day intervals) to check on the moisture in soil and spray with water if needed. Instead of plastic wrapper, you can also use coconut husk with a cotton string tied around it. The husk fibres will bind the soil to the stem.

General Care

☼ Sun

Edibles that we discuss in this book need sunlight in abundance. As explained in Chapter 2 on what your plant needs, the red light in the light spectrum is key for the fruiting and flowering of plants. Since in edibles, our interest is primarily the fruit, these plants need at least 4–6 hours of direct sunlight. Plants such as spinach, arugula or other plants that are grown for leaves can sustain themselves in lesser sunlight (3–4 hours) but will die in the complete absence of direct sunlight.

Temperature

Heat or cold can play an integral part in flower setting for various edibles. If the right temperature is not attained, you won't be successful in your kitchen garden. For example, a tomato plant likes a warm temperature between 20–30°C for flowering and to reach the optimum fruit size. This is neither extremely hot, nor too cold. Any divergence from this range can affect the growth of the plant and act as a hindrance in attaining its full potential. Likewise, lettuce, a winter plant, enjoys 15–25°C as the ideal temperature for full growth. If it's hotter or cooler, either the plant growth will remain stunted, or it may not even germinate from the seed phase. Before growing any plant, one needs to be careful of what temperature it enjoys. In the case of growing edibles, this becomes all the more important because if you don't get successful fruiting, then your entire effort of 2–3 months goes down the drain.

Watering

Thorough and even watering for all edibles is important, particularly for the seasonal kind that grows within a few

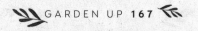

months. Stress from the absence of any of the necessary resources can result in failed plant growth.

🌱 Soil

Edibles are heavy feeders, which means that the potting mix should be compost-heavy. Use fresh, good-quality cattle manure or vermicompost in the potting soil mixed with equal amounts of cocopeat and regular garden soil.

Pot Size

A medium-large pot is ideal for growing edibles. For the shrub kind (i.e., ones that grow up to a metre in height), 12-inch deep pots are good. For gourds that grow as several-metres-long vines, a 14–18-inch deep pot should be used. For fruiting trees, try growing them in the ground directly, but if you do not have that kind of space and you really want to grow that one fruit you absolutely love, use 18–20-inch deep pots/barrels/tubs. Please remember that these pot measurements are for one plant only. I personally tend to cram a lot of plants in small spaces, but it's a bad habit. If you are learning gardening, take note to provide enough space for every plant to grow to its potential. High density of plants in a small space not only makes different plants compete with each other for resources but also makes them vulnerable to diseases and infections. Greed never helps. When you start a plant from a seedling, a 14-inch pot may seem huge for it. However, remember that within a month, it won't be that huge anymore, and, by that time, you might regret your decision of growing two or three seedlings in one pot in order to optimize. Trust me on this!

Issues You May Face

Symptom: White powdery coating

Cause: Powdery white mildew fungal attack

Cure: Use diluted milk (40:60 proportion of milk to water) as a spray on the affected areas of the plant. The milk protein is suggested to interfere in the fungal growth. Generally, optimum air circulation and growing disease-resistant species help deter fungal growth in kitchen gardens.

Symptom: Falling of flowers without fruit formation

Cause: Lack of pollinators and, sometimes, lack of enough nutrition

Cure: Grow pollinator-attracting flowers like marigolds, sunflower, basil and mustard. Additionally, supplement plant growth with regular doses of fertilizer.

Symptom: Stunted growth/yellowing of leaves

Cause: Lack of resources

Cure: Eliminate each resource, such as water, sun and fertilizer, to know which one is causing stress, thereby depreciating the rate of plant growth.

Cause: Leaf-eating insects

Cure: Spray neem oil in the evening (8–10 ml neem oil in 500 ml of water with a few drops of soap solution) on the entire plant.

Ten to Know

Seasonal Edibles

1. Spinach

Suitable Conditions for Good Growth

☼ *Sun:* Partially bright (direct sunlight only in evening or afternoon)
🪣 *Water:* Medium
🧺 *Soil:* Regular potting mix
🌡 *Temperature:* Medium-low
🍴 *Fertilizer:* Not needed if the soil has compost mixed in it

Common Varieties: Spinach (*Spinacia oleracea*) and Malabar spinach (*Basella alba*)

Grow For
- Rich nutrition and quick growth: Fresh spinach leaves and their tender stems are a rich nutrient and mineral source and have anti-cancer and antioxidant

values.* In fact, researchers also suggest that spinach can help prevent Alzheimer's disease.† What makes it even more interesting is that it grows very quickly and can be harvested with in 60 days of starting.

Common Issues

- Poor germination: Try to eliminate the reason which is causing the seeds not to germinate. Figure out if it is the seed quality or you which is hindering the growth of the plant. Ideal conditions for germination are temperatures between 20–30°C, soil which is moist but in which water has not stagnated, and sunlight for 2–3 hours. If all the aforementioned are done or provided correctly, then try again with a new seed or seeds. Seeds exposed to humidity or stored for long can lose their fertility over time.
- Cut or eaten leaves: Leaf-eating insects love feeding off spinach. When you see signs of leaf-eating insects on your plant, let the topsoil dry between waterings and add some wood ash (powder form) around the base of the plant.

Propagation: Start from seeds in soil or pots directly. Plant the seeds 1–inch deep and 4–5 inches apart.

Super Tip: Try a post-workout protein and fibre-rich spinach smoothie. Use 1 cup curd, 1 large bowl of

* J. L. Roberts & R. Moreau, (2016). 'Functional properties of spinach (Spinacia oleracea L.) phytochemicals and bioactives'. *Food & function*, 7(8), 3337-3353.
† W. Jiraungkoorskul (2016). 'Review of neuro-nutrition used as anti-alzheimer plant, spinach, Spinacia oleracea'. *Pharmacognosy reviews*, 10(20), 105.

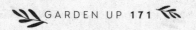

spinach, 1 cup pineapple and 1 cup banana with some ice cubes and blend them together in a mixer.

2. Fenugreek

Suitable Conditions for Good Growth

☀ *Sun:* Bright-partial sun (avoid the afternoon sun)
✎ *Water:* Medium
🌱 *Soil:* Regular potting mix
🌡 *Temperature:* Medium
🍴 *Fertilizer:* Can be skipped

Common Variety: Methi/fenugreek (*Trigonella foenum-graecum*)

Grow For
- Medicinal values and ease of growing: Methi is very popularly used for its medicinal values to treat hair and skin conditions. Studies suggest that the chemical constituents of fenugreek make it anti-diabetic, anti-carcinogenic and an antioxidant. It is also used in treating anorexia.

Common Issues
- Fungal disease: Moist soil conditions can make methi plants susceptible to rot/fungus. Ensure that the potting mix is well draining and add an inch of neem powder on the top of the soil.

- Seeds not sprouting: Ensure that the seeds have not been kept in the open for long (more than a few weeks) as otherwise they may lose their germination ability.

Propagation: Start the plant from seeds directly in a pot or ground, sown 1–2 cm deep and an inch apart.

Super Tip: Methi is a legume, i.e., a plant whose roots capture nitrogen in soil, thereby making it fertile. Therefore, practice crop rotation. Once you have harvested methi, use that soil to grow a heavy feeder plant like tomato.

3. Coriander

Suitable Conditions for Good Growth

- ☀ *Sun:* Bright (avoid the afternoon sun)
- *Water:* Low-medium
- *Soil:* Regular potting mix
- *Temperature:* Medium
- *Fertilizer:* If the potting mix has compost, there is no need to add any more fertilizer

Common Variety: Chinese parsley/dhaniya/coriander (*Coriandrum sativum*)

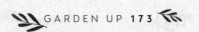

Grow For

- Flavour in food: The tart, lemony taste of fresh coriander leaves can add flavour to any Indian curry or lentils.

Common Issues

- Seeds not sprouting: You can use the coriander seeds for your Indian kitchen spices, but if the seeds have been in the open for several weeks, they may not germinate.
- Leggy and stooping plant: If coriander seedlings are deprived of 4–5 hours of direct sunlight, they will start becoming leggy by stretching their stem to reach out for more light. In such a scenario, the stems also become weak in a few days and start falling on the soil. This increases the vulnerability to fungus, and the seedlings eventually dry and die. The only way to fix this is by ensuring that the plant is getting a lot of sun.

Propagation: Start the plant from seeds in pots or directly in the ground. Sow the seeds 1 inch apart and 1–2 cm deep. Dhaniya takes somewhere between 7–10 days to sprout, so once you have sown the seeds, be patient with germination. Water the soil whenever the topsoil feels completely dry. You can also take out a little soil from a depth of an inch to assess the moisture levels.

Super Tip: For improving the success of your coriander seed germination, wrap the seeds in cotton cloth and beat them with some pressure to open the hard covering.

Before sowing the seeds, you can also soak them in warm water overnight to improve the germination rate.

4. Lettuce

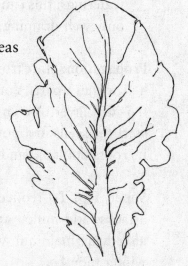

☀ *Sun:* Partially bright (avoid areas that get the afternoon sun)

✎ *Water:* Medium

🌱 *Soil:* Regular potting mix (use good quality, fresh vermicompost in the mix)

🌡 *Temperature:* Low

🍴 *Fertilizer:* Apply a handful of vermicompost per plant at the seedling stage

Common Varieties: Iceberg lettuce (*Lactuca sativa*), asparagus lettuce (*Lactuca sativa var. angustana*), romaine lettuce (*Lactuca sativa var. longifolia asterales*)

Grow For

- Food: A fibre-rich leafy vegetable that can be used in raw form for quick salads and sandwiches.

Common Issues

- Germination failure: Apart from poor seed quality, wrong sowing time of lettuce seeds can also lead to failure in germination. Avoid starting the seeds in the summer or warm season as otherwise the seeds may not germinate. Wait until October at least to sow seeds.

- Wilting and drooping of seedlings*: When the soil is constantly watered without letting it dry between waterings, this can cause rot/fungus in the plant. Use only well-draining, humus-rich soil to grow lettuce.

Propagation: Start from seeds sown 0.5 inches deep and 4–5 inches apart. You can also cover the seeds with a 0.5-inch layer of compost to sow them. If you want to start the seeds in a pot, an 8-inch deep pot is ideal since its roots don't expand very deep.

Super Tip: To reduce exposure to infections and pest attacks, add mulch around the lettuce plant. This will also help maintain warmer soil temperature in cold winter months.

What is Mulch?
Its commonly a layer of organic material and sometimes a plastic sheet added on the top of soil. Its a popular practice in agriculture and horticulture to preserve moisture in soil, reduce weeds, improve fertility and plant growth. Organic materials such as bark chips, saw dust, cocopeat, jute sacks are some known choices as mulch. The process of adding this mulch is called as mulching.

---

* Seedling is the stage when the seed has just germinated with two visible leaves, but when the same plant grows into 4–5 leaves, it is referred to as 'sapling'. A seasonal vegetable seed transfers from seedling to sapling very quickly (within days) while a tree's seedling-to-sapling stage can take relatively much longer (months). These two terms can also be used interchangeably for regular communication in gardening.

5. Beetroot

Suitable Conditions for Good Growth

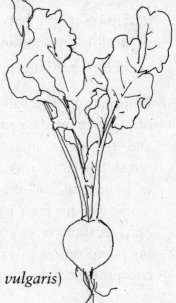

☀ *Sun:* Bright-partial sun
💧 *Water:* Medium
🧱 *Soil:* Regular potting mix
🌡 *Temperature:* Medium-low
🍴 *Fertilizer:* Medium (mixing in potting mix will do the job)

Common Variety: Beetroot (*Beta vulgaris*)

Grow For

- Essential nutrients: Include beetroot in your regular diet for a source of essential nutrients, fibre, potassium, iron and vitamin C.

Common Issues

- Leafy tops but shallow roots: If the soil used for sowing is nutrient rich, especially enriched with nitrogen, then the plant starts investing in its growth above ground, i.e., the leaves, whereas the root growth remains stunted.
- Powdery mildew: Beets need to be grown in open spaces with well-draining soil. If the plants are very tightly packed, or the soil is one in which water constantly stagnates, it makes the plant vulnerable to fungal diseases such as powdery mildew. You can treat the infection by using neem oil solution spray.

However, the harvest may not turn out to be very healthy. So, caution should really be practised at the time of sowing.

Propagation: You can sow the seeds directly in the soil of a pot or in the ground. Bury the seeds 1 inch deep and 4–5 inches apart. Any plant such as beetroot or radish that are grown for their roots should be planted in loose and well-draining soil. Regular potting mix works well for these plants, but if you see that the water remains standing for a few seconds on the soil, amend the composition to improve draining. River sand and cocopeat can help you do that.

Super Tip: For a punch of nutrients, you can include beetroot in salads, smoothies, Indian breads, curries and even desserts such as halwa.

6. Radish

Suitable Conditions for Good Growth

- ☀ *Sun:* Bright
- ♢ *Water:* Medium
- ♆ *Soil:* Regular
- 🌡 *Temperature:* Medium-high
- 🍴 *Fertilizer:* Medium (mixing in potting mix will do the job)

Common Variety: Radish
(*Raphanus Sativus*)

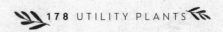

Grow For

- Health benefits and ease of growing. These are fast-growing herbaceous annual plants that are rich in antioxidants, vitamins, minerals and fibre.

Common Issues

- Heavy long leaves but small radishes. For growing such root-based plants, avoid adding nitrogen-rich compost or a fertilizer to the soil. To keep the plant well-nourished and for a balanced growth both above and below ground, use a regular potting mix with equal amounts of cocopeat, compost and garden soil.

Propagation: Sow the seeds 1 inch deep and 4–5 inches apart directly in ground or in large pots (12 inches or deeper).

Super Tip: If you are growing radish in pots, use the dwarf variety seeds.

7. Broccoli

Suitable Conditions for Good Growth

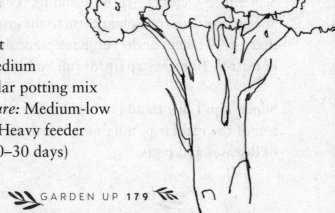

☼ *Sun:* Bright
🖊 *Water:* Medium
🌱 *Soil:* Regular potting mix
🌡 *Temperature:* Medium-low
🍴 *Fertilizer:* Heavy feeder
(once in 20–30 days)

Common Variety: Broccoli (*Brassica oleracea var. italica*)

Grow For
- Nutrition: Broccoli is a winter annual that's recommended for patients with chronic conditions, such as diabetes, and as an immunity booster.

Common Issues
- Seedling failure: If the broccoli seeds start collapsing, ensure that the plant is placed in full-bright sun and the temperature is between 10–25°C. Broccoli also prefers a slightly moist soil. If you are using a regular potting mix, you can increase the amount of loamy or clayey soil in the mixture or keep a close eye on watering. As the topsoil starts drying, add water to keep the soil damp.
- Insects and pests: Plants such as broccoli and cauliflower are vulnerable to worms and flies. As a precautionary measure, you can spray the plant with neem oil solution every 20–25 days. Further, ensure that the soil you are using is insect and pest free.

Propagation: Start broccoli in seedling trays in September–October (early autumn). Once 3–4 leaves appear, you can transplant them to the ground or in pots that are 10 inches or deeper. Each plant should be placed at least 8–10 inches apart for full and healthy growth.

Super Tip: I like to add a 1-inch layer of neem cake on top of the regular potting mix to reduce the occurrence of diseases and pests.

8. Okra

Suitable Conditions for Good Growth

☀ *Sun:* Bright
🖊 *Water:* Medium
🪴 *Soil:* Regular potting mix
🌡 *Temperature:* High
🍴 *Fertilizer:* Medium (add fertilizer during the sapling stage and when the plant starts flowering)

Common Varieties: Okra (*Abelmoschus esculentus*) and red okra (*Abelmoschus esculentus var. red burgundy*)

Grow For

- Ease of growth: Among the fruiting edibles, okra or lady finger is the easiest kind to grow that demands minimum attention.

Common Issues

- Non-blooming: Lack of nutrients or water may lead to non-flowering in okra. Use good quality fertilizer to help the plant flower and fruit.

Propagation: Start from seeds in a sapling tray and transplant during the sapling stage. To start in a pot, use pots which are 10 inches or deeper per plant. If you wish to start in soil, directly sow each seed 1–2 inches deep and 8–10 inches apart.

Super Tip: If you are a beginner and if you want to venture into the world of kitchen gardening, start with growing okra. It's a plant that doesn't succumb to pests, diseases or even watering mess-ups very easily.

9. Tomato

Suitable Conditions for Good Growth

☀ *Sun:* Bright
💧 *Water:* Medium
🪴 *Soil:* Regular potting mix
🌡 *Temperature:* Medium-high
🍴 *Fertilizer:* Heavy feeder
(add fertilizer every 20–25 days)

Common Varieties: Tomato (*Solanum lycopersicum*), cherry tomato (*Solanum lycopersicum var. cerasiforme*), hybrid tomatoes such as Pusa Rohini tomato, Pusa Sadabahar tomato (mostly used in Indian homes for cooking)

Grow For
- Confidence and regular output: For any beginner gardener, tomatoes can be an incredible option to give confidence as they don't die easily and grow fast. Once the plant is established, it will start to flower in clusters, and with the right care, you can get a continuous and good output from the plant.

Common Issues

- No fruiting: The primary reason for flowers drooping without fruit formation is non- pollination. Try hand pollination by tickling the base of the flower for 5–6 seconds every day.

Propagation: Start from seeds between February and May (early spring–early summer). Sow the seeds in seedling pots or trays and transplant to pots which are 8 inches or deeper or directly into the ground, keeping each plant a foot apart.

Super Tip: Grow 2-3 mustard plants around the tomato plant. They grow well as companion plants. Mustard from your kitchen spices can be used to grow around tomatoes. Mustard flower attracts pollinators for the tomato flowers.

10. Gourds

Suitable Conditions for Good Growth

☀ *Sun:* Bright
💧 *Water:* Medium
🪴 *Soil:* Regular potting mix
🌡 *Temperature:* Medium-high
🍽 *Fertilizer:* Heavy feeder
(add fertilizer every 30 days)

Common Varieties: Cucumber (*Cucumis sativus*), bottle gourd (*Lagenaria siceraria*), bitter gourd (*Momordica charantia*), sponge gourd (*Luffa aegyptiaca*), Indian round gourd (*Praecitrullus fistulosus*).

Grow For

- Fast growth. Gourds are vigorously growing, broad-leaved vines that can start fruiting in 2–3 months.

Common Issues

- Powdery mildew: The broad gourd leaves with soft hairs are vulnerable to fungal mildew. You can treat it using any commercial fungicide, diluted milk spray (discussed earlier in this chapter) or diluted vinegar spray. Prepare vinegar spray by mixing 2–3 teaspoons of apple cider vinegar in a litre of water. Spray on the plant in the evening after sunset and wash it off with water in an hour or two.
- No fruiting: Often, gourds produce male flowers before female flowers. If you see the male flowers dropping, it's okay. Female flowers are the precious ones. These flowers are those that will have a tiny cucumber, bottle gourd or bitter gourd growing underneath the flower. If female flowers are dropping without becoming the fruit, that's a problem for a gardener. This indicates that your garden does not have pollinators, such as bees or wasps, to transfer pollen to the female flower. In such cases, hand pollination can help. Snip out a male flower and rub it on the middle section of a female flower. One male flower can be used for pollinating 3–4 female flowers.

Propagation: For home gardeners, you can start gourd seeds directly in a pot or ground. Bury them 1–1.5 inches deep and 8–12 inches apart. For pots, ensure they are 14-inch deep (at least) because gourds like to grow an extensive root system. You can also use old buckets, water dispensers or paint drums to grow gourd vines.

Super Tip: For gourds, always start with a set of 2–3 seeds at a time, and, within a season, grow a few such sets in a staggered manner (at least 20–30 days apart). This is done so that if one plant is producing only male flowers, you can use them to pollinate female flowers on another plant. Given the chronology of flower production on a plant (males before females), growing multiple vines simultaneously and multiple sets of such vines in a season will increase your chances of pollination.

Ten to Know

Perennials

1. Mint

Suitable Conditions for Good Growth

- ☀ *Sun:* Bright to partial sun
- 🜄 *Water:* Medium
- 🜨 *Soil:* Regular potting mix
  (ensure that it's well-draining)
- 🌡 *Temperature:* Medium-low
- 🍽 *Fertilizer:* Low (once in 5–6 months)

Common Varieties: Water mint (*Mentha aquatica*), spearmint (*Mentha spicata*), peppermint (hybrid of water mint and spearmint), pineapple mint (*Mentha suaveolens* 'variegata')

Grow For

- Flavour in drinks, food and ease of growing: Mint, because of its refreshing smell and taste, is popularly grown as a herb used in salads, pastas, chutneys, ice creams, *raitas* and also in drinks such as julep, mojitos and green teas, to name a few. It is a hardy perennial that can flourish if the growing conditions are right.

Common Issues

- Drying of the plant: Mint loves cool and moist conditions, and any diversion from that can lead to slow drying of the plant. Although it likes to be watered frequently, remember to let the topsoil dry between waterings. Constant saturation of soil air pockets with water can limit the plant's growth, thereby causing blackening of leaves and rot as well.
- Failure with stem cutting propagation: Sometimes when the cutting with roots is transplanted from the water to the soil, it tends to droop and dry. To get better success with stem cuttings, I recommend starting with 5–6 cuttings at one go. Additionally, when you add the cutting to the soil, keep the pot in semi-shade conditions for at least 3–5 days unless

you start noticing new leaf growth on the stem (which is an indication that the stem has successfully established itself in the new soil).

- Spreading as a weed: Some species of mint start taking over the garden if not contained or if no root barrier is used. In order to avoid mint from competing against other plants, try growing it in a pot or a container.

Propagation: Starting from seeds as well as stem cutting method works for the plant.

Super Tip: Peppermint is medicinally used to ease the bowel muscles for better digestion, treat cold and flu and also lower blood sugar in diabetic patients.

2. Basil

Suitable Conditions for Good Growth

☀ *Sun:* Bright
💧 *Water:* Medium
🪴 *Soil:* Regular potting mix
🌡 *Temperature:* Medium-high
🍴 *Fertilizer:* Medium

Common Varieties: Holy basil (*Ocimum tenuiflorum*), sweet basil (*Ocimum basilicum*), Thai basil (*Ocimum basilicum var. thyrsiflora*)

Grow For

- Exotic cooking, medicinal values and ease of care: I prefer growing herbs like basil and mint because you don't have to wait for the flower to use them as an edible—you can pluck the leaves and use them any time. Among the three kinds of basil mentioned above, sweet basil and Thai basil are popularly used in pastas, quiches, soups and seasoning, while the third kind—holy basil—is popularly used in medicines and teas. Holy basil or tulsi can be used in case of common cold, influenza, bronchitis and general fever.

Common Issues

- Fungal problem: Basil is prone to fungal attack, especially either when there is infrequent watering or the sunlight available for the plant is not enough. Any powdered form of fungicide can be used to treat the plant, but this treatment is not a permanent solution unless watering and sun condition aren't improved.

Propagation: Start basil from seeds in seedling pots and transplant each plant to a pot that is 8 inches or deeper.

Super Tip: For continuous good growth of basil, don't allow the plant to flower. Whenever you start noticing flowers or buds, pinch them off in order to encourage the plant to grow more leaves. However, if you have plenty of basil growing, you can let them flower as they attract pollinators to the garden.

3. Curry leaf

Suitable Conditions for Good Growth

☼ *Sun:* Bright-partial sun
✎ *Water:* Medium
🌱 *Soil:* Regular potting mix
🌡 *Temperature:* Medium
🍴 *Fertilizer:* Medium
(every two–three months)

Common Variety: Curry leaf/curry patta
(*Murraya koenigii*)

Grow For
• Flavour and medicinal values: The alkaloids (kind of chemical components) in curry leaf makes it not only smell and taste wonderful, but also makes it a wonderful medicine. It is antibacterial, anti-inflammatory and acts as a sugar regulator for diabetic patients.

Common Issues
• Spots under the leaves: Fungal attack causes black and sometimes white spots underneath or on top of curry leaves. To reduce its vulnerability to fungus, avoid watering the plant from top and add water only to the soil. For treatment, you can use a store-bought fungicide.

Propagation: Stem cutting with rooting hormone method.

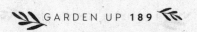

Super Tip: My curry leaf plant grows best under the partial shade of larger trees. The bigger plant's canopy can help filter the sun and reduce its intensity, thereby helping the curry leaf plant flourish.

4. Chilli

Suitable Conditions for Good Growth

- ☼ *Sun:* Bright
- *Water:* Medium
- *Soil:* Regular potting mix
- *Temperature:* High
- *Fertilizer:* Medium

Common Variety: *Capsicum Frutescens* and *Capsicum annuum* (**Commercial varieties commonly sold in India are Jwala, Kanthari, Kashmiri chilli, G-4 variety and TNAU hybrid chilli Co1**)

Grow For
- High fruit production: Chilli and capsicum (also a kind of chilli actually) flower often. Hence, they are among the veggies that can give you more fruit.

Common Issues
- No fruit: If the flowers are blooming but not turning into a fruit, that is an indication of lack of pollinators. You can try hand pollination with the help of a paintbrush.

- Curling of leaves: Chilli leaves are delicate and prone to heat stress. Curling leaves can be a sign of too much heat or be an indication that it is too windy for your plant. Try moving the plant to a partially bright area, and in case the plant can't be moved, use shade cloth that can filter sunlight.

Propagation: Start plant from seeds in a seedling tray or a moist tissue paper. Once the seeds have germinated, transfer the plant into a pot of 8 inches or deeper or plant in soil directly.

Super Tip: Use chillies to pickle them, which allows storing them for longer periods when the plant yields good fruit. Both dried and green chillies can be used for pickling.

5. Rosemary

Suitable Conditions for Good Growth

☀ *Sun:* Bright
💧 *Water:* Medium
🪴 *Soil:* Regular potting mix
🌡 *Temperature:* Medium
🍴 *Fertilizer:* Medium (once in 2–3 months)

Common Variety: Rosemary (*Rosmarinus officinalis*)

Grow For

- Ease of growing: Rosemary is a hardy evergreen plant that grows with minimum attention, especially in the Mediterranean climate where the temperatures are between 15–35°C and the sun is bright.

Common Issues

- Root rot: Constantly moist soil can cause rotting of the roots. Use a well-draining soil to grow rosemary.
- Mealybugs: Use a soap solution spray in the evening on the affected parts and wash off with regular water next morning.

Propagation: Start from seeds in seedling trays and transplant them in 6–10-inch deep pots or directly in soil, at least 8–10 inches apart.

Super Tip: Use mulch around the plant to reduce the negative effects of extreme weather conditions on the plant.

6. Brinjal

Suitable Conditions for Good Growth

☼ *Sun:* Bright
💧 *Water:* Medium
🪴 *Soil:* Regular potting mix
🌡 *Temperature:* Medium-high
🍴 *Fertilizer:* Heavy feeder
(add fertilizer every 20–30 days)

Common Variety: Eggplant/brinjal/baingan/aubergine (*Solanum melongena*). Within this species, some commonly cultivated varieties are classic large brinjal, black beauty brinjal and Thai green brinjal.

Grow For

- Ease of growing: If the plant receives all the basic needs—i.e., sun, soil and water—in the right amounts, it will not trouble you with anything else. Of course, adding fertilizer can enhance fruiting and fruit size, but, even without that, if you have good pollinators in your garden, brinjal will keep giving you fruit.

Common Issues

- Reduced flowering and fruiting: Even though it's a perennial, it gives a good output of fruit only for one season. The fruiting and flowering falls drastically after a year.

Propagation: Start from seeds in a seedling tray and transplant the seedlings to a pot which is 10 inches or deeper or plant in soil at least 8–10 inches apart. You can also sow directly in pots or in the ground, but with seedling trays you will be saving time and energy for seeds that don't germinate for reasons beyond your control.

Super Tip: Grow the plant against a wall to protect its broad leaves from intense winds or sun. Any factor that increases the rate of evaporation causes a quick drooping of leaves in brinjal plants.

7. Pomegranate

Suitable Conditions for Good Growth

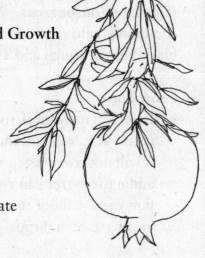

☀ *Sun:* Bright
🖌 *Water:* Medium
🌱 *Soil:* Regular potting mix
🌡 *Temperature:* High
🍴 *Fertilizer:* Medium feeder

Common Variety: Pomegranate
(*Punica granatum*)

Grow For

- Juicy fruit and aesthetics: Pomegranate tree bearing the red-orange juicy fruits can be a perfect ornamental addition to your garden.

Common Issues

- Insect and fungal attack: This warm climate-loving tree can be vulnerable to nymphs and mould, thereby making the plant weak and surrender to the infestation. As a precaution, spray neem oil solution every two months on the plant, especially when you see any kind of insects multiplying in number. Constant inspection of the leaf's underside and branches can help keep a check on the infection status.

Propagation: You can start the plant from seeds initially in small pots or seedling trays if you do not have space

available immediately. However, eventually you will have to move the plant to at least a 14-inch deep pot or to the ground. For pomegranate seeds, use a potting mix with compost, cocopeat/river sand and garden soil in equal proportions.

Super Tip: Regular pruning of side branches and dead parts can help the plant flower and fruit faster.

8. Banana

Suitable Conditions for Good Growth

☼ *Sun:* Bright
✎ *Water:* Medium
✎ *Soil:* Regular (use nitrogen-rich compost in the potting mix)
🌡 *Temperature:* Medium-high
🍴 *Fertilizer:* Heavy feeder (once every two months)

Common Variety: Bananas were at first divided into two species, but with a large number of varieties cultivated across the globe, scientists did not find that classification helpful for the purpose of identification. In India, the *Musa* is a popular variety that is widely cultivated. Within this species, there are over ten subspecies or varieties that are grown in the farms of India. Some easy-to-grow varieties are dwarf cavendish, robusta, Singapuri, monthan and champa, to name a few.

Grow For

- Nutrition-rich fruit: Banana is an easy-to-grow fruiting plant that is a rich source of vitamins, fibres and minerals.

> #FUNFACT: *For a banana plant, flowering and fruiting takes at least 9 months. When the plant dies at the base, you will see something known as the 'corm', and around this corm you will observe more plant pups growing out. Additionally, people often refer to banana plants as a 'tree', but it's more of a perennial herb than a tree. Trees are identified with a woody single trunk that goes up to a considerable height, none of which you see in banana plants. However, don't get mixed up in the nomenclature. It's all good as long as you know how to care for the plant.*

Common Issues

- Banana wilt: Among the many bacterial and fungal diseases that affect the banana plant, one very prolific is a soil-based fungus which causes what is referred to as the 'Panama disease'. It is very common in tropical regions where you find the right conditions to grow bananas. This fungus invades the roots attacking the plant's young parts, thereby causing the browning of leaves. The most effective defence to this disease is to grow varieties that have become resistant to this disease. While purchasing the seeds or seedlings, look for disease-resistant varieties available locally.

Propagation: From the mother plant, remove the pups that have a few roots, and repot them in a new pot. Home gardeners can purchase a rooted and potted plant from the nursery directly.

Super Tip: Bananas make a great windbreak for the garden. You can plant them on the periphery of the garden. Additionally, their leaves can be used to feed cattle, and, therefore, they are of great use to people developing a farm. Each part of the banana tree can be put to some use.

9. Lemon

Suitable Conditions for Good Growth

- ☀ *Sun:* Bright
- ✎ *Water:* Medium
- 🌱 *Soil:* Regular potting mix (ensure that the compost you are using in the mix is phosphorus rich)
- 🌡 *Temperature:* High
- 🍴 *Fertilizer:* Heavy feeder (add fertilizer every two months)

Common Varieties: Lemon/nimbu (*Citrus limon*). Lemons are suggested to have been first grown in

India, specifically Assam, as well as in parts of Burma and China. In India, some common varieties that are currently popularly grown are the Assam lemon, pan lemon and Malta lemon.

Grow For
- Vitamin C: An easy-to-grow plant that bears a wonderful concentrated packet of vitamin C, an immunity booster, along with a range of other vitamins and minerals.

Common Issues
- Pests and disease: Overwatering can make lemon plants vulnerable to rot and insect attack. Lemons can withstand underwatering to some extent, but overwatering will definitely bring your plant down. This plant likes to be regularly and evenly watered.
- Yellowing of leaves: Apart from irregular watering, yellowing of leaves can be caused by nutrient deficiencies. Use nitrogen- and phosphorus-rich fertilizer for lemon plants, especially just before the flowering sets in.

Propagation: Lemon plant can be started from a cutting, from seeds as well as by layering. For a beginner, I would recommend getting a prepared plant from a plant nursery.

Super Tip: Lemons are more sensitive to cold than to heat. Adding mulch around the plant in the extreme winters (under 10°C) can help protect the plant.

10. Guava

Suitable Conditions for Good Growth

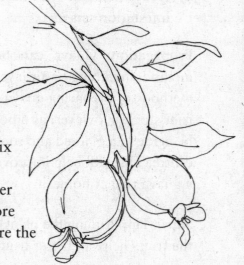

- ☀ *Sun:* Bright
- ◊ *Water:* Medium
- 🌿 *Soil:* Regular potting mix
- 🌡 *Temperature:* High
- 🍴 *Fertilizer:* Medium feeder (add fertilizer once before the rains and once before the onset of winters)

Common Varieties: Guava (*Psidium guajava*). Some other common varieties that are commercially grown are Sardar, Allahabad Safeda, Lalit, Bengal Safeda and Pant Prabhat. A few hybrid varieties have also been developed, such as Lucknow-49, Safed Jam, Kohir Safeda and Arka Amulya.

Grow For

- Fruit: Guava fruit is rich in calcium, phosphorus and vitamin C. A guava tree also attracts birds to its fruits. Planting fruit trees help to give a mini forest feel to any garden.

Common Issues

- Insects: Guava plant often gets infected with fruit flies, thrips, nematodes and mealybugs. To treat them, it's a good practice for a home gardener to

spray the plant with neem oil solution whenever an infestation sets in.

Propagation: Guava can be grown by the budding method, inarching or air layering. These are commercial methods of preparing guava plant cuttings to develop a root stock. However, as a home gardener, I recommend bringing in a planted and rooted cutting from the garden centre. This will help improve your success with starting a guava tree at home.

Super Tip: Pruning the plant once a year after harvesting the fruits helps in better fruiting in the next season.

4.2 MEDICINAL PLANTS

Historically, medicinal plants have played a pivotal role in human life. Long before the evolution of modern chemistry, humans used plants based on their instincts, taste or smell to treat ailments. Today, the interdisciplinary field, combining phytochemistry, plant biology and evolution, has aided in expediting our understanding of medicinal compounds in plants. According to the National Medicinal Plant Board (NMPB) of India, out of the 17,000–18,000 flowering plants found across the country, a whopping 35% have been documented for their medicinal properties in the traditional Indian system of medicine. This includes literature from Unani, Ayurveda, Siddha, homaeopathy, Sowa-rigpa (Tibetan medicine) and other ethno-botanical literature.* What

---

* D.K. Ved and G.S. Goraya, "Demand and supply of medicinal plants in India," *NMPB, National Medicinal Plants Board, New Delhi* & *FRLHT Foundation for Revitalisation of Local Health Traditions, Bangalore,,* India 18 (2007) Link: http://www.secondaryagriculture.org/agri-researchdata-book/frlht.pdf.]

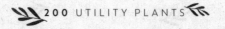

makes it more interesting to me is that the assessment reported by the NMPB suggests that 25 per cent of the medicinal consumption in the country is non-commercial, in the form of botanical raw drugs.

Medicinal plants that you can grow in your small window or a terrace have been and can be conveniently used for minor flus, fevers and even for general well-being. Within this plant category, tulsi or holy basil (*Ocimum tenuiflorum*) is the first one to come to my mind (and possibly yours too). So, let's talk about it. Beyond the wisdom of our elders, scientific facts and lab results of the chemical composition of tulsi make this Indian household plant quite appealing. Its various extracts and forms, ranging from dried powder of leaves to essential oil, are shown to have immunomodulatory, anti-inflammatory, analgesic, radioprotective, anti-tumourous, anti-toxic, hypoglycemic and hypolipidemic properties.* Basically, it is truly a champion herb.

These scientific derivations are not only made from chemical analysis of the composition, but also from trials conducted on humans. Such studies compared the medicinal effect of tulsi on human health recovery to controls (humans who were not given the tulsi derivative). Today, therapeutically, tulsi is popularly used for treating hepatic disorders, lowering of blood

---

* Amit Kumar et al., "Ocimum sanctum (Tulsi): a miracle herb and boon to medical science—A Review," *International Journal of Agronomy and Plant Production.* 4.7 (2013): 1580–9.

sugar levels, as a heart tonic, and for its antioxidant and anti-stress properties, among many other uses.

It must be said, though, that what you read here is not medical advice or prescription but a simple statement of facts based on research about the benefits of an easy plant that you could be growing at home. Please consult your physician for any medical advice.

Beyond tulsi, there are many other plants that hold medicinal values and are commonly used to treat various skin diseases, the flu and gastritis, while others are used for balancing sugar levels in the body and general well-being. Here, I share with you a list of such plants, arranged in order of ease of growing them for home gardeners:

Please treat whatever you read here as gardening advice, not medical advice.

Ten to Know

Medicinal Plants

1. Aloe vera

Suitable Conditions for Good Growth

☀ *Sun:* Bright
💧 *Water:* Low
🪴 *Soil:* Regular potting mix
🌡 *Temperature:* High
🍴 *Fertilizer:* Low

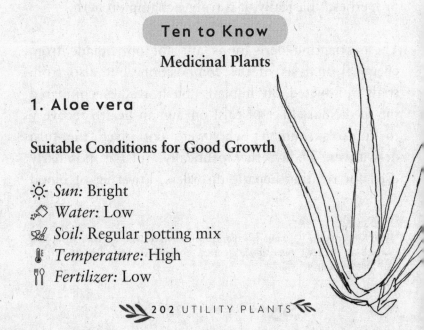

Common Variety: Aloe (*Aloe vera*). Specifically, the variety known as *Aloe vera barbadensis miller* is edible.

Grow For

- Ease of growing and medicinal properties: Aloe is an extremely easy-to-grow plant that offers a wide range of benefits to the human body. To name a few, it might help in lowering blood sugar, reducing constipation, healing wounds and treating burnt skin.

Common Issues

- Soggy leaves: It is a succulent that cannot stand overwatering. Water deprivation is not a problem for aloe, but frequent watering will irritate it and the leaves will become moist and soggy. To save the plant from watering issues, if you are a beginner, uproot the plant and check the topsoil. You should add water only when the soil is completely dry. There is no fixed frequency that can work for everyone for watering succulents. Soil inspection can help you learn how quickly or slowly the soil dries in your area. In my west-facing Mumbai balcony, I water my aloe vera plant only once a week.

Propagation: Remove the pups with a few roots and repot them in a new pot.

Super Tip: Add river sand to the regular potting mix for growing aloe vera. This will improve drainage and reduce the chance of plants dying from overwatering.

2. Giloy

Suitable Conditions for Good Growth

☀ *Sun:* Bright partial sunlight
🖊 *Water:* Medium
🪴 *Soil:* Regular potting mix
🌡 *Temperature:* High
🍴 *Fertilizer:* Low

Common Variety: Giloy vati (*Tinospora cordifolia*)

Grow For
Ease of growing and medicinal properties. It's a large, broad-leaved vine that likes to grow on a tree.

Common Issues
- Starts growing as a weed: Regular pruning of giloy is important to contain the plant, as otherwise it can take over your entire garden, making it difficult for other plants to grow.

Propagation: Growing from a cutting works best for giloy.

Super Tip: Try to grow giloy on a neem tree. It's called 'neem giloy' where giloy is believed to take on the medicinal values of neem as well.

3. Tulsi

Suitable Conditions for Good Growth

☼ *Sun:* Bright
🔆 *Water:* Medium
🪴 *Soil:* Regular potting mix
🌡 *Temperature:* Medium-high
🍴 *Fertilizer:* Medium feeder

Common Variety: Tulsi/vrinda//holy basil
(*Ocimum tenuiflorum*)

Grow For
- Medicinal properties: Therapeutic value* of tulsi has been documented from age-old ayurvedic, Roman, Greek and Unani scriptures to modern medical research papers. We have already dedicated some space to this.

Common Issues
- Fungal attack: Lack of enough sun makes tulsi susceptible to fungal attack. Ensure that the plant gets sunlight for 5–6 hours.

Propagation: Start from seeds.

---

* Deepika Singh and Prabir K. Chaudhuri, 'A review on phytochemical and pharmacological properties of Holy basil (Ocimum sanctum L.),' *Industrial Crops and Products* 118 (2018): 367–382.

Super Tip: Pinching off flowers from the plant helps tulsi to continue growing vegetatively and become bushy from a single stem.

4. Neem

Suitable Conditions for Good Growth

☼ *Sun:* Bright
◇ *Water:* Medium
🪴 *Soil:* Regular potting mix
🌡 *Temperature:* High
🍴 *Fertilizer:* Medium feeder

Common Variety: Neem (*Azadirachta indica*)

Grow For: Medicinal properties and ease of growing

Common Issues
- **Slow Growth:** In the initial phase of growth, it develops slowly for 2–3 years. Once the stem becomes woody, the plant gains speed in growth and will start bearing fruit from the third to the fifth year. A neem tree can have a productive life for over a hundred years.

Propagation: Cutting with rooting hormone

Super Tip: Neem leaves can be dried and saved in powder form, which can then be used for minor skin infections, burns and even as a mouthwash.

5. Ginger

Suitable Conditions for Good Growth

- ☼ *Sun:* Bright-medium
- *Water:* Medium (sparse watering when you have just sown and generous watering once the shoots emerge from the soil)
- *Soil:* Regular potting mix (well-draining)
- *Temperature:* High
- *Fertilizer:* Low feeder (use good quality vermicompost in preparing the potting mix so that you don't have to add fertilizer anytime later)

Common Variety: *Zingiber officinale*

Some common varieties include but are not limited to IISR Varada, IISR Mahima and Suruchi. For a home gardener, the variety that you get in the grocery store is good enough. Only the developed green eyes are important for planting.

Grow For
- It is a hardy plant with medicinal values and is used as a common spice in Indian food

Common Issues: Rotting of the rhizome

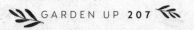

Propagation: Start using a budding ginger rhizome where you can see a green/yellow eye. Place the 2-3 inch rhizome 2 inches deep and 6 inches apart in a loose loamy soil potting mix.

Super Tip: If you wish to grow ginger in a container, be mindful of the season. It likes to grow in summers, starting in May. However, a heavy monsoon can be disturbing for the plant. During the monsoons, move the plant in a space with some kind of a roof to protect the soil from stagnant water build-up. You can store sun-dried thin slices of ginger for longer. They can also come handy for making tea and in cooking.

6. Turmeric

Suitable Conditions for Good Growth

- ☼ *Sun:* Bright
- *Water:* Medium
- *Soil:* Regular potting mix (well-draining)
- *Temperature:*
- *Fertilizer:* Medium (use good quality fertilizer in the potting mix at the beginning)

Common Variety: *Curcuma longa.* Some common Indian varieties are Erode Local, Alleppey Finger, Rajapore, Sangli turmeric, Rajapuri, Madras turmeric, BSR-1, PTS-10, Roma etc.

Grow For: Medicinal value. It is also a hardy plant.

Common Issues: Rot and fungal attack on the rhizome.

Propagation: Bury the rhizome 2–3 inches deep and 6 inches apart in well-draining soil. You can cover the rhizome with pure compost as well instead of soil. Start the plant in summers.

Super Tip: Before harvesting, let the part of the plant above ground die out completely. This will let the rhizome develop completely and attain its flavour.

7. Garlic

Suitable Conditions for Good Growth

- ☼ *Sun:* Bright
- *Water:* Medium
- *Soil:* Regular potting mix (well-draining)
- *Temperature:* Medium-low
- *Fertilizer:* Medium (use good quality fertilizer in the potting mix at the beginning)

Common Variety: *Allium sativum*
There are two species of garlic as for food: soft-neck (*Allium sativum*) and hard-neck (*Allium ophioscorodon*). Within these species, some of the varieties, which include but are not limited to Bhima

Omkar, Bhima Purple, Yamuna Safed and Agrifound Parvati, grow well in India. However, if you are a home gardener, just use the cloves from your grocery bag and don't bother with the name of the variety.

Common Issues: White rot on the leaves.

Grow For: Its hot and spicy taste and ability to promote healthy digestion.

Propagation: Start growing during autumn. Use the biggest cloves of garlic available. Plant with the root side towards the soil and the upper part facing the sky. Bury each clove 2 inches deep and 6 inches apart.

Super Tip: Mulch the top of the soil with sawdust, grass cutting or dried leaves. This process will help suppress the growth of weeds.

8. Lemongrass

Suitable Conditions for Good Growth

- ☀ *Sun:* Bright-partial sun
- 💧 *Water:* Medium
- 🪴 *Soil:* Regular potting mix
- 🌡 *Temperature:* Medium-high
- 🍴 *Fertilizer:* Medium (once in 4–5 months)

Common Variety: West Indian lemon grass (*Cymbopogon citratus*), East Indian/ Malabar/ Cochin lemon grass (*Cymbopogon flexuosus*).

Grow For: Ease of growing and medicinal properties.

Common Issues: Yellowing and drying of leaves.

Propagation: Start from seeds or pups from a large plant.

Super Tip: If you have a garden, start lemongrass in the ground as a fence. It will also out-compete most weeds in the ground. Further, if you have a lot of lemongrass growing, you can use it as a nitrogen-rich balm around all kinds of plants.

9. Ajwain

Suitable Conditions for Good Growth

- ☼ *Sun:* Bright-partial sun
- ◇ *Water:* Medium
- ✄ *Soil:* Regular potting mix
- 🌡 *Temperature:* Medium-low
- 🍴 *Fertilizer:* Medium
  (once in 4–5 months)

Common Variety: Carom/ajwain (*Trachyspermum ammi*)

Grow For
- Medicinal properties and flavour for Indian food.
- Use the seeds for consumption.

Common Issues: Yellowing of leaves and slow growth

Propagation: Start from seeds directly in a pot or in the ground by burying the seeds 1 cm deep and 5–6 cm apart. The plant prefers low temperatures, so start growing in autumn.

Super Tip: Do not confuse ajwain with Mexican oregano that smells quite like ajwain. Actually, the ajwain plant's leaves do not smell like the seeds at all.

10. Ashwagandha

Suitable Conditions for Good Growth

- ☼ *Sun:* Bright-partially bright sun
- *Water:* Medium-low
- *Soil:* Regular potting
- *Temperature:* Medium
- *Fertilizer:* Medium feeder (once in 4–5 months)

Common Variety: Ashwagandha (*Withania somnifera*)

Grow For
- Medicinal properties. Various parts of ashwagandha are used in dried, powdered form.

Common Issues: Aphids, mites and rot.

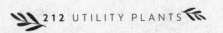

Propagation: Start the plant from seeds in seedling trays (bury an inch deep) and transplant after a month in soil, placing the plant 8–10 inches apart. Keep the soil on the drier side while sowing the seeds and even during transplanting. Ashwagandha does not appreciate wet feet at all. The plant will be ready to be harvested in 150–180 days.

Super Tip: Ashwagandha gives a good harvest if the climate where the plant is grown is suitable. It does best in high-altitude areas (~1500 metres above sea level).

Notes

PART III

Bonus Unlocked

Chapter 5
GARDEN PLANNING

Before you start out to set up a garden or become a plant parent, I recommend spending some time thinking about some questions you must ask yourself.

a. What is my budget? You may not enjoy sitting down with a pen and paper to do the calculations, but it is important to set realistic goals of spending money.

b. Am I looking for a seasonal garden or a permanent garden? Seasonal garden needs planting and investment every few months, while a permanent garden needs major investment and efforts upfront, followed by regular pruning and inspection.

c. How much space do I have available? Is it a balcony, a plot or a window that you have available for gardening? Plan accordingly.

d. What are the weather conditions in my area? Identify the temperature, humidity fluctuations and sun availability between seasons and within a day.

e. What are the native species or plants that grow easily in my region? Growing a coconut tree in

Himachal Pradesh will not work out, just as growing strawberries will not work out in Mumbai. Therefore, considering native species can help get successful results in the garden.

f.   Do I want to accessorize my garden? Setting up a space to enjoy the garden is as important as looking after the plants. Try thinking of ways that give you space to enjoy your fruits of labour.

g.   What is your motive to start a garden? Is it to meet your food needs, to have a little oasis in your house or a hobby to divert your mind?

The size of the garden, the number of plants and their type depend upon the answers to these questions. If you are an absolute beginner, start with two to three plants. Pick any kind and see how you feel about nurturing them every day. Growing plants and attending to them may feel demanding for some while being very relaxing for others.

Notes

○

○

○

○

Chapter 6

COMMON TERMS

In this chapter, I've collated terms you might come across on your plant parenting journey.

a. Aerobic: A process that takes place in the presence of oxygen or air (loosely used). For decomposition of waste for the purpose of composting, you need to regularly aerate the mixture for a faster result.

b. Anaerobic: A process that takes place in the absence of oxygen.

c. Aquaponic gardening: Growing of plants (mostly edibles) in water in the absence of any soil and using fish to provide nutrients for plant growth.

d. Chlorosis: Yellowing of plant leaves due to the loss of chlorophyll that has been caused by infection, disease, water stress or nutrient stress.

e. Cold frames: A transparent-roofed, enclosed space used for growing plants in cold places. A cold frame can be considered as a mini greenhouse that helps to retain heat in cold weather, especially during the night.

f. Cottage garden: An English-style garden where the place is densely decorated with flowers, ornamentals and edibles in an informal fashion.

g. Crop rotation: A farming practice where a crop is not repeated sequentially in the same plot for two consecutive seasons. This is shown to be an effective way to reduce pest load, optimize nutrient availability and improve overall crop harvest.

h. Double dug bed: A gardening method where the topsoil layer is removed, thereby exposing the sub-soil (12–18-inch section of soil) which is then topped with manure or compost. This method improves root growth and water drainage, thereby helping in an overall better growth of the plants.

i. Grafting: A gardening technique where the upper part (scion) of one plant grows on the lower part (root stock) of another plant. This method is popularly used for fruiting trees like guava, jamun, mango, etc. It helps in reducing the time for the first flower and fruit production. Grafting is generally used for imparting disease resistance and high yield quality from one plant (root stock) to another (scion).

j. Hardening: A process of making plants acclimated to the new environment when they are moved from one place to another. It is generally used for saplings that are started indoors and then planted outdoors.

k. High tunnels: These are transparent, enclosed farmlands, constructed in order to improve plant growth and provide a longer growing season for the farmers. They are very similar to a greenhouse, except that in a greenhouse, there is a heating source and the plants are grown in pots that are eventually to be moved out. In a high tunnel, plants are sown in the ground and will complete their life cycle within them.

l. Humus: A soil component formed from decayed plant material.

m. Hydroponic gardening: Growing of plants in a soil-less medium in water and the provision of nutrients artificially for plant growth.

n. No-till garden: A garden where the gardener does not till to loosen the soil. This technique of gardening relies on regular mulching and manure/compost addition to the soil. It has been reported to be beneficial for the plant growth as tilling is found to break fungal networks in soil, thereby helping in improving soil health.

o. Permaculture: A term that comes from 'permanent agriculture' and relies on sustainable practices of growing plants. It relies on 12 commonly accepted principles for usage of any land:
- Observe and interact.
- Catch and store energy.
- Obtain a yield.
- Apply self-regulation and accept feedback.
- Use and value renewable resources and services.
- Produce no waste.
- Design from patterns to details.
- Integrate rather than segregate.
- Use small and slow solutions.
- Use and value diversity
- Use edges and value the marginal.
- Creatively use and respond to change.

p. Scarification: The process of opening the seed to germination through mechanical pressure, thermal exposure or chemical treatment. For example, coriander seeds need to be mechanically beaten with some pressure before being sown in soil as otherwise they won't germinate.

q. Square foot gardening: Gardening method of dividing the growing space in square-shaped sections to effectively and intensively use it for plants. Here is a list of edibles that can be grown using the practice of square foot gardening to get the best output from your kitchen garden.

Area	Number of individuals	Plants that can be grown
1 sq. ft.	1	Chillies, cabbage, cauliflower, tomatoes, brinjal, rosemary, curry leaf, okra
2 sq. ft.	1	Gourds, pumpkin, melons, cucumber
1 sq. ft.	2	Basil, coriander, mint, oregano, tulsi, most herbs, lettuce
1 sq. ft.	3	Ginger, garlic, turmeric, beans, lemongrass, ajwain
1 sq. ft.	6	Radish, carrots, spring onions

r. Vertical gardening: A gardening style that emphasizes usage of vertical space for plants. Accessories like plastic panels, fabric hanger with pockets and plastic pouches hung on metal frames make vertical gardening easy and manageable. One can grow a variety of ornamental as well as food plants in a small space through vertical gardening. They are also referred to as 'green walls'.

s. Worm casting: A result of decomposition of organic material by worms. Scientific evidence shows that worm castings are a rich source of nutrients for the plants.

t. Xeriscaping: A landscape design that relies on reducing the water dependence to a bare minimum. It includes growing plants that can sustain in the water naturally provided in that habitat and without artificial watering or irrigation. This landscaping method has picked up in popularity in drought-prone areas around the world.

Notes

Chapter 7

GARDENING FOR KIDS

I have many young cousins ranging from 5 years to 18 years of age, and the spark that I see in them every time a seed they have sown sprouts is priceless. Beyond a hobby, gardening can be a lesson in patience and persevering through failure. A mustard seed sown from your Indian kitchen will sprout in the first week, large broad leaves will follow in 30 days, followed by bright yellow, beautiful flowers in 45 days. Each phase of a plant's growth is a treat for the eyes and soul. Watching a plant's life cycle gives a sense of accomplishment. A mustard seed (Indian rai) which your child, niece or nephew may have never noticed before starts blooming within a month of growing it in a kilogram of soil, and bees soon start visiting the plant. It swirls with blowing wind and reminds us how with some patience and a little bit of effort, one can turn that boring black seed into a fun vibrant flower.

Here are a couple of gardening projects on growing food from your kitchen that I have tried with children in my workshops with schools.

PROJECT 1

Patience Level: Low

Requirements: 8–10-inch deep and >6-inch pot, any kind of soil you have access to and 5–10 fenugreek (methi) seeds or 5–10 mustard seeds or 5–10 carom (ajwain seeds)

Season: Winters or whenever the temperature is not above 35°C

Method

i.   Block the drainage hole at the bottom of the pot by pressing an inch of soil against it. This will allow only the water to escape and retain the soil in the pot.

ii. Fill the rest of the pot with the soil up to 1.5–2 inches from the top of the pot. This vacant space on the top of the pot will help water to sit and not overflow as you start watering your plant. While filling the pot with soil, don't try to press or make it condensed. Avoid clay-heavy soil as it becomes compact very quickly.

iii. Make a few 2–3-cm-deep wells in the soil with your index finger and add 1–2 seeds per well. Keep a minimum of 5–6 cm distance between the wells and cover them with soil.

Sunlight: Direct sunlight for 4 hours minimum

Watering: Whenever the top inch of soil is dry

Expectations: If you want to enjoy the fruit of your efforts quickly, harvest the plant on the seventh day of germination and use it as a microgreen. If you have a little more patience, wait for 30–45 days when the leaves are 4–5 inches deep and use them to cook saag or sabji. If you can bear just a little more time, both mustard and methi will start fruiting in 50–70 days and the flowers will grow pods that will have seeds in them. This way you can enjoy the entire life cycle of a plant, from seed to seed.

PROJECT 2

Patience Level: Medium

Requirements: 8–10-inch deep and >6-inch diameter pot, any kind of soil you have access to and one tomato slice (less than a centimetre thick)/2–3 seeds from a red chilli (fruit not powder)

Season: Whenever the temperatures are between 20°C–40°C

Method

i.   Follow Steps (i) and (ii) of Project 1.

ii. Place a slice of tomato on the soil or 2–3 chilli seeds and cover with 0.5–1 inch of soil. If the slice of tomato gets exposed to water, gently press it deeper.

Over the course of 7–10 days, the seeds in the tomato slice will germinate, and you may notice the red pulp portion decaying; it's completely normal. We are not interested in the pulp. With chilli seeds, you will not encounter any such issues. In case more than two seeds sprout in one pot, you can remove the extras and plant them in a different pot. This should be done when you see at least 4-5 leaves in each sapling.

Sunlight: Direct sunlight for 5–6 hours minimum.

Watering: Whenever the top inch of the soil is dry

Expectations: You should find the seeds germinating into cotyledons in the first 6–7 days. If that doesn't happen, either you need to try with a different set of seeds or you are watering it wrong. We have talked about these issues in great detail in the previous chapter, so you can try again. In 30–40 days, the plant will reach a height of a few feet and in another week or so, it will start flowering. Since both tomato and chilli flowers grow male (pollen) and female (ovaries) parts together, wind pollination should help the flower become a fruit. The plant will last for 3–4 months and continue giving fruit or rather the fruit of your labour.

PROJECT 3

Patience Level: High
Requirements: 12–14-inch deep and >10-inch diameter pot, well-draining soil that you have access to and 1

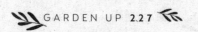

large bulb (each clove separated) of garlic (lehsun) or lobe of ginger (adrak) with green eye/s.

Season: Start post-rains/monsoon

Method

i. Follow Steps (i) and (ii) of Project 1.
ii. Make a 1–2-inch deep well in the soil and place one clove of garlic or tuber of ginger and cover with soil. Maintain a minimum distance of 3 inches between two wells.
iii. Add a fertilizer or compost every 30–40 days.

Sunlight: Direct sunlight for 6 hours minimum

Watering: Only when you are sure that the top 1–2-inch layer of soil is dry, because overwatering will start rotting the sown tuber or clove and you wouldn't even know.

Expectations: In 9–10 months, the leaves of the plant will start drying and yellowing, indicating that the plant has matured and is ready to be harvested. The one rhizome (of ginger) or one clove (of garlic) would have divided into many at the base of the plant.

Lastly, try to enjoy the process of gardening, even if you fail. It may feel disappointing, but remember that nobody is born with a green thumb!

Notes

ACKNOWLEDGEMENTS

Writing a book was the last thing on my mind. I never thought I could be an author. But this journey has been very fulfilling as it helped me to overcome the fear of things that I believed I was never capable of conquering. It was only when I was half-way through writing this book that I realized this was perhaps the best way of structuring and sharing my thoughts and learnings from academia and my hands-on gardening experience.

My editors at Penguin Random House India—Tarini Uppal, who played a significant role in convincing me to take up writing, and Shaoni Mukherjee and Angana Moitra, who have helped with the edits and re-edits—have made publishing this book possible.

When I started 'Garden Up' as a YouTube channel, my first source of strength was my audience. I could not believe that people actually found my suggestions and advice useful. They gave me the confidence to embark on a relatively lesser traveled path of social media instead of pursuing a faculty position after my PhD. My decision to leave a socially celebrated profession was questioned and doubted by many close to me. Surely, they wished the best for me. But it was the Garden Up audience who truly cheered me on and helped me build something completely from scratch. I am thankful to everyone who has watched, shared or followed my work. I may not know your name, or might not have ever met you, but you have helped a girl believe that she could do what she wanted to!

My mentors from Indian Institute of Science, Professor Sukumar, Dr Pascal Jouquet, and the faculty inculcated the habit of scientific thinking in me. It has changed my approach to the smallest or simplest things that I do. Dr Joquet was an integral part of all my research publications and helped me with edits of my academic writings. It's from him that I learnt how scientific communication can be simply worded, thorough, yet not intimidating. I hope I have been able to apply some of that knowledge in this book.

I am truly grateful to my team at Garden Up—Neha, Joice, Subham, Upasana and the many interns who have been with us on the journey so far. I lean on them for so much. Through the course of writing this book, I was not as available to them as I should have been. But they graciously took up more responsibilities and were always very excited and supportive of this project.

I am thankful to my parents and my Naani (my grandmother), who believe in me and support me even when they do not always understand my actions and my decisions; to my parents-in-law and my family, who make me feel special and loved. To my younger brother, Arjun, who lends a patient ear when I need it. He has dedicated countless hours from his college break fixing my garden, setting up the irrigation system and de-weeding my plants. Thank you to my entire immediate and extended family and friends, who take great interest in my work and are my cheerleaders forever.

And, finally, to my husband, Pulkit, my biggest supporter, my biggest critic and a true partner in everything that I do. He is the only person who was more enthusiastic about this book than I was. He read, suggested edits and re-read every page of the manuscript till it was perfect for him. He was and remains my drive and my motivation.